D1109783

BETWEEN THE LINES

Warner Books, Inc., 1271 Avenue of the Americas, New York, NY 10020

Visit our Web site at www.twbookmark.com

For information on Time Warner Trade Publishing's online publishing program,
visit www.ipublish.com

A Time Warner Company

Printed in the United States of America
First printing: September 2001
10 9 8 7 6 5 4 3 2 1

Library of Congress Cataloging-in-Publication Data

Hershiser, Orel.
Between the lines : nine principles to live by / Orel Hershiser with Robert Wolgemuth.
p. cm.
ISBN 0-446-52850-1
1. Baseball players—Religious life. I. Wolgemuth, Robert D. II. Title.

BV4596.B37 H64 2001
796.357'092—dc21
[B] 2001026328

Book design and text composition by L&G McRee

"He
Lov
"W
(A
Fl
C

BETWEE
THE LINE

Nine Principles to Live By

OREL HERSHISER
WITH ROBERT WOLGEMUTH

WARNER BOOKS

A Time Warner Company

To Jamie, Quinton, and Jordan.
I'll never grow tired of your love.
I'll never stop loving you.

ACKNOWLEDGMENTS

This book is filled with the names of many people—family and friends. As you read you'll find out that their contribution to my life—and the principles—has been huge. This book is an expression of sincere appreciation to them and a recognition of their gifts to me. My sincerest thanks to each one.

A special thank you goes to Robert Wolgemuth, one of my closest friends for more than twelve years. Writing this book with him has been a great experience. A fellow German eccentric, Robert didn't mind my brooding over every single word.

And a big thanks to my wife, Jamie, who carefully edited the first draft of the manuscript.

Also thanks to Jo Ann Lacey and her colleagues, who did the transcribing so efficiently and accurately.

The folks at Warner Books/Nashville—Rolf Zettersten, Leslie Peterson, Paul Shepherd, Kathie Johnson, and Preston Cannon—caught the vision for this book in the first place. Their encouragement and professional skills have made it happen. Also thanks to Larry Kirshbaum, Jamie Raab, Maureen Egen, Martha Otis, Chris Barba, and Jimmy Franco and their colleagues at

Warner Books/New York for their support. Also, thanks to Ken Samuelson, my friend the detail wizard who made sure that every baseball stat was correct.

Finally, a special thanks to Dixie Fraley. Her friendship means so much. Her husband, Robert—my sports representative for seventeen years—meant more to me than I could ever express. The pages that follow are meant to be a tribute to both of them.

CONTENTS

FOREWORD

When I found out that Warner Books was publishing a book by Orel Hershiser, I called them myself and told them I wanted to write the foreword. They didn't ask me to do it. I offered.

Why did I call the publisher? Because I love Orel Hershiser and I want you to read this book and get to know him, too.

For over three decades I have managed some pretty remarkable people, including the talented young athletes of the 2000 Olympics gold-medal-winning baseball team. As a result, I have had the privilege of shaping and molding the talent and mettle of some of the best athletes in the world. Orel Hershiser is one of those at the top of my list. Let me tell you why.

The first time I met Orel was when the Dodgers brought him up in the fall of 1983. He was an impressive young man. And I knew the moment I met him that this was a man of great character. The following spring in Vero Beach, I could tell he was ready. There was a skill, a focus, and an aggressiveness that I liked. So I sent him out to pitch. But a few weeks into the regular season, I noticed a tentativeness. A fearfulness. Instead of trusting his instincts, Orel was out there trying to make the perfect pitch.

I had had enough. I told Ron Perranoski, my pitching coach,

to bring Orel into my office. I really read Orel the riot act. I got in his face and told him he had good stuff but that he was afraid. He was pitching negatively and he didn't believe in himself.

"Go after the hitter," I said. "Quit being so careful. Get ahead of the count. Even the good hitters are going to fail 70 percent of the time. You got what it takes to get *anybody* out."

What I saw in Orel over the next twelve years was a baseball player with a tenacious will to learn, to grow, and to improve. I saw an outstanding young man who was a hard worker—aggressive, even daring, on the mound. Not only did I get what I asked for, I got *more.*

Without a doubt, Orel Hershiser is one of the smartest baseball players I've ever managed. His intelligence is visible on and off the field. He's a gentleman. He loves God. He loves his family. Orel's the real thing. Since that day back in 1983 when I first met him, we've become like father and son. I loved him as a manager and today I love him as a friend.

Orel's a man who deserves the title *role model.* I tell people, "If you have children, just hope they grow up to be like Orel Hershiser. If you have a daughter and someone like this comes to date her, invite him in, lock the door, and never let him leave!"

Everyone needs someone like this to look up to. Orel Hershiser is one of the best.

If you ask Orel a question, he'll tell you the truth. At all times. And that's exactly what he's done in this book. If you want great advice about living from someone who has the right to speak, you've come to the right place. Orel was a shrewd player on the field—a tireless student of the game of baseball. But I have as much respect for his perspective on the game of life. Even though Orel Hershiser is a sports hero to many, this is not a book about baseball. It's a book for people who want to live balanced, productive lives. People like you and me.

If you knew Orel Hershiser like I know Orel Hershiser, you'll read this book and do exactly what it says.

TOMMY LASORDA

PREFACE

A Quiet Table Back in the Corner

During the summer of 2000, when I retired from pitching in the big leagues, the folks at Warner approached me about writing a book. I told them that I wasn't interested in writing an autobiography. I'm too young for a book like that. So they suggested that I string some of my stories and experiences together, using them as a backdrop to help someone out of a tough situation or to encourage and inspire a friend who needed a lift. Someone like you.

We decided to call the book *Between the Lines.* Of course, as a baseball player, I know the feeling of stepping across the foul line on my way to the pitcher's mound from the dugout. At that moment, everything I've prepared for from the time I was a little boy comes into sharp focus. And the anticipation of putting this into play is awesome. It still makes my heart race when I think about it.

Stadiums fill up with people to see what's going to happen between the lines.

But life isn't only about visible realities. There are invisible and unseen nuances. These subtleties are shaped by our experiences, by our families, and by our culture. And there are events—a lot of them unplanned—which become part of our own personal histories. These things change us and shape us into who we are. A big part of my life and yours is this unseen but very influential stuff. The part that hides *between the lines.*

What I've done in this book is taken some of my life experiences—events you may have read about in the paper and many you haven't read about—and boiled them down into nine principles that are very important to me. I hope they will be helpful to you, too.

Actually, this isn't a book at all. It's a conversation.

My good friends know that when I'm in a comfortable setting with people I enjoy, I love to tell stories and laugh and listen.

Many of a big leaguer's conversations are with reporters who choose the questions. Video cameras and microphones pick up every word they speak. Although I've enjoyed a good relationship with the media for almost twenty years, that isn't the comfortable setting I'm talking about.

No, this one's different. I get to choose the topics and pick the questions. And instead of staring into bright lights, I'm relaxing with someone I enjoy talking to.

So if you and I were able to sit down right now, I'd tell you my stories, then I'd ask you about important people and times in your life—and what makes you tick. You'd tell me about your family and their influence on you. You have experiences in your past that would make us laugh. Or you may have stories of when you were faced with some kind of a serious illness or the loss of a job. Maybe the love of your life walked away or one of your children disappointed you.

Since it's not possible to actually sit face to face, we're going to have to imagine that you and I are sitting in a booth way back in the corner of some old diner where the ceiling fans turn slowly. I'm going to tell you some of my stories and what I've learned from them. We've been here many times before. This restaurant is like an old friend. The dark "wood-grain" Formica on the tables is worn through to the white on the edges and the smooth, shiny vinyl on the benches is occasionally interrupted by pieces of gray duct tape to keep the stuffing from popping out. Of course, our waitress—the one who calls everyone Honey—will interrupt us, take our orders, bring the food, and occasionally refill our coffee cups. We'll say thanks and then pick up where we left off.

You and I have a lot to talk about and this is a perfect place to do it.

PRINCIPLE #1

Believe Your Coaches

It would have been bad enough if just one of these things had dropped on me. But having them happen at the same time was more than I could take. It was time for something radical.

Cars and trucks zoomed past me as I stood on the shoulder of the I-75 entrance ramp, less than a mile from the entrance to BG (Bowling Green State University). The wind whipped through my hair and tugged at my jacket. I squinted from the dust that kicked up in my face. Standing there with my thumb in the air, hoping for a ride, I had never felt this hopeless. Never.

Of the three reasons why I had gone to college—to get an education, have fun, and play baseball—I was failing in all three. It was my first time away from home and I wasn't doing well. Running away seemed logical for a guy in my situation.

Academically I was in serious trouble. It was final-exam week and I knew I wasn't going to get a passing grade in a single subject. Living in a noisy dormitory, trying to get myself up every morning, hitting the snooze button too often, and missing lots of classes had brought predictable results. Why bother to take the stupid tests?

Socially, I felt like a loser. My girlfriend had just broken up with me. She wanted us to "still be friends." Maybe my disappearing from school would make her feel so terrible that she'd take me back. I hoped it would.

It might have been possible to survive the bad grades and the broken heart, but the real crusher was getting cut from the baseball team. This was the reason I had gone to BG in the first place. It was what I'd lived for.

No passing grades, no girlfriend, and no baseball. Miserable didn't come close.

I scribbled a clever note to my roommate, leaving a hint as to where I was going. I guess I wanted to make a statement and have people chase me, find me, comfort me, and help me to start over. An eighteen-year-old in my condition doesn't completely want to run away and cut all the strings. But a guy with any pride at all didn't just walk up to his parents or his friends and say, "Look, I'm a failure. I have no excuses. Can you help me?"

Taking off like this, I felt a strange mix of fear and excitement. I'd never pictured myself as a rebel, but I needed to do something rebellious. Something bold. I decided that running away would attract attention to my pain and maybe detract attention from my failure. I had blown it, big time, and I didn't want to face the consequences of my losses and poor decisions. So I stuffed my duffel bag with an extra pair of jeans, a couple of shirts, some underwear, and my Dopp kit, and walked out of my dorm.

Without a car of my own, hitchhiking was my transportation of choice. And with a face that looked more like Opie from Mayberry than Charles Manson, I had no trouble getting rides. A mother with a car full of kids picked me up first. Brushing crackers and a couple of toys to the floor, I made a spot on the backseat.

Another young mother gave me a ride, telling me that she never picked up hitchhikers but thought I looked like a "decent young man." Unfortunately, she only took me to the next exit. *I need a long ride,* I thought to myself as I crawled out of her car and stuck out my thumb. *I haven't even made it out of Ohio.*

A huge truck, spewing exhaust from giant chrome pipes, slammed on the brakes, the tires laying down a long black skid. I ran along the shoulder to catch up to the truck. With the smell of burning rubber still coming off the tire marks on the road, I climbed in.

I'd never been in the cab of an eighteen-wheeler. "Yo, buddy," the driver laughed, sticking out his hand. I shook it. This guy wouldn't have been afraid of anyone.

Pulling back onto the highway he looked at me and smiled. Most of his teeth seemed to be in place. "You like Charlie Pride?" he asked, working on a wad of bubble gum the size of a golf ball. "Yes, sir," I lied. Heading east on the Ohio Turnpike and doing sixty-five was more important to me at the time than telling the truth. At the Pennsylvania line, he was turning south toward West Virginia. He pulled over and stopped. I crawled down from the cab and thanked him for the ride. I really meant it.

> No passing grades, no girlfriend, and no baseball. Miserable didn't come close.

In just a few minutes, a traveling salesman picked me up. He moved a pile of papers from the front seat to the back, and I got in. After a few minutes of quiet, he tried to ask me about myself. I was evasive. Then he told me that he was a born-again Christian. I nodded, like I was interested in hearing more. He talked nonstop and I tried to act like I was listening. He kept talking and I kept nodding. Charlie Pride or Jesus aside, at least I was going home to New Jersey.

HOMECOMING?

Right after my senior year in high school, my family had moved from Cherry Hill, New Jersey, to the Detroit area where my dad had accepted a partnership in a large printing company. But home for me was never going to be Michigan, so I'd decided I was going back to New Jersey. I guess I thought there would be banners across Main Street, welcoming me home like some war hero. (What was I thinking?)

So I kept heading east. For the moment, it was my only goal.

A guy about my age stopped to pick me up. Except for his nonstop smoking, I didn't pay much attention to him. He had a nice car and I liked the aggressive way he drove. We hardly spoke at all, which was fine with me. In fact, I don't think we made eye contact once. Unfortunately, as he was whipping around a big truck on the right, another truck was merging into the same lane and we slammed into the back of it. A wreck was not something I had expected but it was a perfect illustration of how I felt about my life. I couldn't even hitchhike right.

The interview with the state trooper didn't go well. Technically, hitchhiking was against the law, especially on an interstate highway. "Uh, you know, uh . . . I'm a student, just getting a ride and I don't even know this guy's name and, uh . . ."

I guess I didn't look like a typical hitchhiker with my preppie haircut and clean clothes. The trooper asked me a few more questions then let me go. Of course, I couldn't just stick out my thumb and start hitchhiking right in front of him, so I started to walk along the shoulder.

With only the sound of the gravel crunching under my shoes a sense of complete despair came over me. "What am I doing?" I said out loud. *Okay, now what? I'm out here in the middle of nowhere with nothing but a few bucks and some clothes. I graduated from Cherry Hill East but all my friends are gone. They're not home waiting for me. And what am I going to do when I get back there?*

Stand in front of people I know and tell them I'm a failure? Tell them I went off to college but I couldn't hack it?

I can't describe how empty I felt. *I guess this is what rock bottom feels like.*

The sun was setting. Soon it would be as dark outside as I was feeling inside. I wasn't so brash that I was going to stand along the side of the road through the night, so I snagged one more ride then started looking for a motel—a motel with a telephone.

"Dad, this is Orel," I said, faking some bravado. My dad was ready for my call. Jeff, my roommate, had called my parents to tell them I had run away.

"Oh, you've really done a number on your mother now." His voice was stern and strong and his words hit hard. I'd never wanted to disappoint my mom. Realizing what I was putting her through made me feel terrible. My dad might as well have said, "Oh, Orel, look what you've done. You're not even considering what you are doing to anybody else; you're just thinking about yourself." He would have been right.

> The boy on the bus to Michigan was not the man I wanted to be.

Dad was good in a crisis. He was angry, but completely under control. I was relieved because I knew deep down he was happy that I was safe.

"Get on a bus," he said. "Come home and we'll talk about it when you get here."

After spending the night in a motel, I boarded a Greyhound bus bound for Detroit. As a baseball player, bus trips were very familiar. I knew the fun of riding a bus home celebrating a big victory and I knew the pain and loneliness of riding a bus after a loss. But this bus ride was one I would never forget. It followed the biggest defeat I had ever known. My parents had tried to instill in me a will to hang in there—to persevere, regardless of the outcome. But I had given up. When the going got tough, I ran away. And even worse than my dad's stern voice and my mother's broken heart, I was disappointed in myself.

The boy on the bus to Michigan was not the man I wanted to be.

COACH DAD

As I look back on this experience more than two decades later, it is perfectly clear to me that this was a watershed moment, a fork in the road. The impact of those who had "coached" me during my childhood was now being challenged by the harsh reality of growing up. Would the words and examples of these mentors hold or would self-pity and failure swallow me up? Would I decide to deal with the truth and do the right thing?

> "If you're going to live here, you're going to work and then you're going back to school."

I'd like to tell you that as the bus drove from somewhere in Pennsylvania to Detroit, I sat there paging back through these things that brought me to this moment. Actually, I wasn't that introspective. All I really did was stare out of the window and think about how hard it was going to be to face my family, especially my mom. I was the oldest of four kids, and I didn't feel like a responsible big brother. Some role model I was.

I tried to sleep.

Finally, the brakes hissed our arrival in Detroit. For me, this was the end of the line. A small group of people began gathering around the bus. Stepping down onto the sidewalk, I scanned the crowd, looked around for a familiar face. But no one had come to meet me. I knew it was my dad's way of letting me know that, although he loved me, he wasn't going to coddle me or treat me like a child.

He was very wise in knowing just how far to push before I would break. "Let him go," I can remember him saying to my mom when I faced failure as a young boy. "He's got to learn."

Having a welcoming committee at the bus stop would have sent the wrong message. I looked around for a taxi, crawled in the backseat, and gave the driver my parents' address.

A strange mix of fear and relief surrounded me as I stepped out of the cab. It was great to be home. This was not a familiar house but it didn't matter. It was the people inside I had come to see. Hugs from everyone made me feel much better. The smell of something good was coming from the kitchen. But before I sat down to enjoy my first home-cooked meal in weeks, my dad let me know, "If you're going to live here, you're going to work and then you're going back to school." He wasn't angry, but true to his German roots, he spoke with unwavering resolve. I didn't argue. I knew better than to argue.

THE TACKLE BOX

As I look back over my growing-up years, I realize how perfectly suited my dad was to me. His sternness made sure that my failures taught me important lessons, but he was always there for me when there was an emergency.

Like the time my friend Jack Rex and I decided to drive to Florida for spring break. At twenty, we were old enough and barely smart enough, if you know what I mean.

Rather than budgeting our money for the week, we spent too much on the drive south and too much on things we didn't really need during the first few days. Soon Jack and I were counting change on the bed, hoping to have enough to keep gas in my Camaro Z28 for the trip north. I thought of phoning my dad for some help, but didn't want to admit we had been foolish enough to run out of money.

We went to the grocery store and bought a loaf of bread, some peanut butter, and a plastic knife. Sitting on the bed in our hotel room and eating sandwiches, I called home and told my parents that everything was going great. Pride is a powerful thing.

Sure enough, we had budgeted just enough gas money to get home. Sprawled out on the family room floor, I was soon laughing and telling stories to my siblings and parents about Jack's and my adventures in Florida. After a few minutes of fun, I finally admitted, "Hey, I'm starving."

Sheepishly, I then told them how we had almost run out of money and admitted that I had been too proud to ask for help. I looked at my dad and saw a big smile on his face. "Go get your tackle box," he told me.

"What do you mean, go get my tackle box?" I replied.

"I said, go get your tackle box," he said again with a twinkle in his eye.

I dutifully went out to my car and retrieved the tackle box that had made the trip to Florida and back.

> Growing up was an endless sequence of being overlooked by the in crowd and having a hard time making friends and good grades.

"Open it up," my dad said as I set it down on the family room floor. I obeyed, still wondering what he was up to. With my family gathered around, I felt like I was on display.

"Look under the tray," he said, once the box was opened. I reached under the tray filled with lures and found an envelope taped there. I pulled the envelope free and tore it open. Two crisp one hundred dollar bills fell out. Everyone laughed. I laughed, too, amazed that my dad had taken good care of me, even when I didn't know it.

"LITTLE O"

Even though I passed my dad in size a long time ago, I will always be "Little O" to him. And Orel Leonard Hershiser III was not only my dad but my first great coach. He was a competitor from the word "go." I saw that in his business life, when he played cards with his friends or when he raked the infield before one of my Little League games. He was never satisfied with the status quo, so I saw him push himself toward perfection. And he held up the same standard for me, my sister, Katie, and my two brothers, Gordie and Judd. A Saturday of cleaning the garage was not just an ordinary chore, it was an exercise in the pursuit of perfection. Dirt and clutter were enemies to be conquered.

As his oldest son, I inherited this same competitive spirit—every bit of it. And, as it turned out, I was going to need it.

NOT A MEMBER OF THE "IN CROWD"

Several weeks ago, while dropping one of my sons off at school, I saw lots of kids huddled together in the parking lot, laughing and joking. Then I saw a couple kids off by themselves, wishing they could be included. My heart was drawn to those kids because, as a youngster, that had been me.

Everyone my age was bigger and more mature than me. Growing up was an endless sequence of being overlooked by the in crowd and having a hard time making friends and good grades. I was the last to shave, the last to have a steady girlfriend, and the last to drive a car. I felt like an alien, trying to figure out how to survive in a world where I wasn't up to par in size, academic strength, or social skills.

But, deep down, my dad's tenacity connected with me. I remember admiring his ability to finish what he started and his commitment to doing his best.

"Average may be good enough for other kids," he might as well have been saying to me, "but you're not other kids. You're *my* son." Although, of course, I didn't select this man to be my dad—my first coach—I did choose to watch him and listen to his advice. I wanted to be like him.

During these years I also always heard the sound of my mom's voice cheering me on. A good coach and an enthusiastic cheerleader—what else could a skinny kid named Orel Leonard Hershiser IV ever need?

GRANDPA SANDWICHES

As my first coach, my dad planted a competitive spirit in me, but (he still doesn't like to hear me say this) I probably didn't get my athletic ability from him.

Our first home was in Buffalo, New York. We lived just a few miles from a man who became another one of my early coaches—my maternal grandfather, Harry T. Gillman. Grandpa Gillman's influence on me was profound.

He wasn't a large man but Grandpa Gillman was a gifted athlete. As a young man he had excelled in swimming, golf, and baseball. The war and his dad kept him from pursuing a career in sports. Actually, during the thirties and forties, professional athletes were not admired—or paid—like they are today. Often men went into professional sports as a last resort rather than a career.

From the time I was old enough to slip my hand into a baseball glove, Grandpa Gillman played catch with me in his backyard. At lunchtime we'd go into the kitchen and he'd make me a ham-and-cheese sandwich with lots of mayonnaise and spicy mustard. He called them "Grandpa sandwiches" and they tasted awesome. A sandwich is always better when someone else makes it for you, especially someone you love. Ham-and-cheese sandwiches, baseball, and lots of love. Grandpa Gillman was the best.

Sometimes Grandpa took me to the drugstore and bought me comic books. Back home we'd play Chinese checkers and Parcheesi with the board spread out between us on the floor.

Grandma made me soft chocolate-chip cookies and let me eat them between meals. In their backyard, I played by the hour. Grandpa would make a circle in the dirt with his finger and show me how to shoot marbles. And I would play catch with him—he taught me how to hold the ball, how to step and throw—and, when he got tired, I'd toss the ball up against the fence . . . over and over and over again. They never told me to stop.

Grandpa Gillman introduced me to golf at the age of five. After school he would take me out to the Lancaster Country Club and we'd play two or three holes before Grandma joined us for dinner. Between ordering dinner and the time the food arrived, I'd go to the putting green until they'd call me in to eat. Sometimes after dinner I'd go back to the putting green again. If it hadn't been for the light on the corner of the greenskeeper's shack, it would have been pitch black. This was no problem at all.

> A sandwich is always better when someone else makes it for you, especially someone you love.

But sports wasn't Grandpa Gillman's only specialty; he was also a great life-skills coach. I can remember watching how he treated people with dignity and respect. The consummate gentleman, I saw how he cherished Grandma. He thanked people constantly, even those who didn't expect it. I can picture how he acted when he and I would take his car in for service, leaning over the fender next to the mechanic. "Wow, I would never have seen that," he would say. Not only was he honoring the mechanic, he was right in there, watching and learning. Grandpa was a student of the people around him. He was always involved.

Absolutely no one was beneath this man. When a serviceman made a call to his house, Grandpa would offer him lunch, then sit down with him and eat sandwiches he or Grandma had made.

Grandpa was a student of the people around him. He was always involved.

On some weekends when my parents worked part time for a retail pharmaceutical company, inventorying drugstores, Grandpa and Grandma Gillman took us to the Central Presbyterian Church. I can remember the sounds of the church service, the smell of the old wooden pews, and the feeling of sitting in the big sanctuary. I can especially remember listening to the music. And I remember standing between my grandparents when the offering plates were brought forward, singing the Doxology.

Praise God from whom all blessings flow.
Praise Him all creatures here below.
Praise Him above ye heavenly hosts.
Praise Father, Son, and Holy Ghost.

There was something very special about those moments. Standing between these people I loved and being filled with wonder at the sound of this hymn. These memories helped to shape my heart.

WALKING TALL

Dave Martin was the varsity baseball coach at Cherry Hill East High School. As a freshman with dreams of making the varsity team, I can remember passing him in the hallway. Hoping he'd notice me, I'd straighten up and try to walk tall. And I worked harder than the rest of the boys in gym class. Coach Martin was a man's man—a man who hadn't lost his athletic prowess. He may have been a little rough around the edges, but he had a big heart. He was a hard worker who loved his students and the school he worked for. Loyalty was a big deal in his book. Even though he was in the athletic department and not seen as an academic giant, he always spoke highly about the school and seemed to be well liked by the other teachers.

Coach Martin was a gentleman. He taught us to treat girls properly and, as far as I could tell, he lived a life of order and principle.

He also had high standards when it came to picking his varsity team. In the spring, there was only one baseball tryout—for the varsity team. As a freshman, this was all I wanted. Years of Little League and youth baseball had prepared me for this tryout. For the guys who weren't good enough to make the varsity, there was the junior varsity (JV) team. But for those who lacked the skills for either, there was the freshman team. A couple of my friends made varsity, a few more the junior varsity. I made neither and spent the season playing shortstop and pitching on the freshman team.

My sophomore year I tried once more. Coach Martin cut me again, but this time he put me on the JV team. Finally, the next year, with my dad's work ethic and my Grandpa Gillman's talent, I made the varsity team, although I wasn't a huge contributor.

A couple of my friends made varsity, a few more the junior varsity. I made neither.

Then, in my senior year, it happened. My body and skills caught up with my will and I made it as a starter. I was one of the team leaders, selected as all-conference in South Jersey, and I saw my name in the local paper on a regular basis. My parents were very proud.

Coach Martin continued to have my respect as an important coach, and now he was becoming my friend. I would visit his office between classes or drop in on him instead of going to study hall. He was often busy grading papers, but he'd take time to talk baseball or college possibilities with me. Sometimes we'd go outside and I'd help him get the field ready for a game.

But baseball wasn't the only thing he cared about. I can remember Coach Martin telling me to be sure to finish my homework. Even though I know he saw some potential in me as a baseball player, he wanted me to be a complete person. He also knew that actually making a living playing baseball was a long shot, a very long shot.

A CHANCE AT THE BIG LEAGUES

But let's get back to my story. Once the dust had settled from my running away from college and my return to my parents' home in Detroit, I enrolled in summer school back at Bowling Green. The campus during the summer months was a different place. There were fewer activities, fewer friends to call . . . fewer distractions. It was exactly what I needed and my grades showed it.

After summer school, I played on a team that won the All-American Amateur Baseball Association national championship. I was the starting pitcher in the title game. By my junior year at BG, I had grown three inches and gained fifteen pounds. The speed of my fastball had picked up five miles an hour and I made the school's traveling team.

> I knew this call was the real thing. No one would joke about something like this.

During that season, BG coach, Don Pervis, and I were approached by local big league scouts. I had seen them in the stands with their radar guns and clipboards and I hoped they were looking at me for the June 1979 amateur draft. I was right.

On the night of the draft, I sat in my apartment staring at the telephone, praying it would ring. It did. The man on the line told me that he was with the San Diego Padres and he was taking me in the first round. I was ecstatic. I couldn't believe it. I called my dad and he couldn't believe it either!

After a few phone calls to my friends, I began to smell a practical joke. Their guarded enthusiasm was a tip-off. Sure enough, my fraternity brothers had made the call, not the Padres. I laughed and acted like I could take the joke, but inside I was crushed.

The next day, the real call came. It was from the Los Angeles Dodgers and I was being taken in the seventeenth round—I knew this call was the real thing. No one would joke about something like this.

In a few weeks Boyd Bartley, a Dodger scout, came to our home in Detroit to present their offer. Because I wasn't going to turn twenty-one for three more months, my dad had to be in the meeting. Mr. Bartley offered me ten thousand dollars, an assignment, and a dream. "We'll send you to our Class A team in Clinton, Iowa. You'll have the chance to grow and develop and work your way up the ladder to play in the big leagues. We want you to pitch in Dodger Stadium some day."

I was awestruck by his words. My dream was about to come true. I was going to turn pro. After a short meeting in the kitchen with my dad and mom, I took the offer.

The next four years would be a blur of playing baseball in some pretty interesting places: Clinton, Iowa; San Antonio, Texas; Albuquerque, New Mexico; and a few winter ball stops in Scottsdale, Arizona; Valencia, Venezuela; and Santo Domingo, Dominican Republic.

NOW THE WORK BEGINS

Six different cities and four and a half years in the minors and the call came.

At the end of the 1983 season, after finishing third in the Pa-

"You've made it to the big leagues. But the work has just begun."

cific Coast League in saves and seventh in earned run average (ERA), I was called up to the big club—the Dodgers. My first role was in the bullpen and I finished the season with eight innings pitched in eight different games in relief. I did well the next spring and made the club out of camp for the 1984 season.

The following spring, my wife, Jamie, and I found a rental house in Placentia, forty-five minutes to an hour and fifteen minutes from Dodger Stadium, depending on the traffic. Because we only had one car I needed to find a teammate who lived in the area and who could drive me to the park when I needed a ride.

Burt and Ginger Hooton lived close by and Burt agreed to let me ride with him. He was a soft-spoken Texas guy. One of the veteran starters, Burt was known for his overhand fastball, knuckle curve . . . and strong character.

And on those long drives to Dodger Stadium, Burt Hooton became a good friend—and coach. Since he was unwilling to shake his Texas musical roots, the radio provided a backdrop of country music most of the time, but I'm not about to tell a guy who's giving me a ride that I don't like his music.

It brought back memories of that awful hitchhiking trip from Bowling Green, but the music was the only thing that was the same. Everything else was different. Instead of running away from college, riding through Ohio in an eighteen-wheeler, I was a big leaguer, riding along with a veteran big leaguer. Imagine the awe of sitting there, soaking in the wise words he spoke. Because Burt was not a small-talker, there were times when five or ten minutes of complete silence would go by. But when he had something to say, it was always something worth listening to.

Just like Grandpa Gillman did with his mentors, I pumped

Burt with questions and soaked in all his answers. I had questions about work ethics and strategy and the Dodger coaches and the day's opponent. My friend always filled me in. It was great.

But on one of those rides to the ballpark, Burt said something I never forgot. It sealed him as one of my most important coaches. "Orel," he began between my questions and Hank Williams, "You've made it to the big leagues."

I could tell he wasn't finished, so I sat quietly.

"But the work has just begun. It took a lot of work to get to the majors. But when you got here, you took someone else's job. Now everyone is going to want your job. It was hard to get here but it's going to be even harder to stay here."

In the years that followed, these words became profoundly true.

"BULLDOG"

In my book *Out of the Blue* I told the story of when my first major league manager, Tommy Lasorda, gave me the nickname "Bulldog." It was May of 1984, my first full year in the majors. I've often referred to the meeting in his office as "The Sermon on the Mound." Because he had been told to, Ron Perranoski, my pitching coach, escorted me into Tommy's office. I was carrying a 2-2 record and my ERA was a miserable 6.20. I knew I could do better than that and suspected that Tommy agreed. I was glad that Perry had come along—although Tommy wouldn't have met with me, or any of his players, without their coach present.

No person had ever been more intimidating to me than Thomas Charles Lasorda. He was an enthusiastic leader, but although I had not played for him for more than a few months, I also knew that he was loud and brash. Verbally, he took no prisoners. A few days before this meeting, I had given up a two-out double in Houston to José Cruz with two men on base. Tommy was furious. But his anger was not directed at my mechanics or pitch selection. He was mad at me because he thought I was pitching timidly and didn't believe in my abilities.

Now I was sitting in his office. "You don't believe in yourself," he shouted. "You're scared to pitch in the big leagues! Who do you think these hitters are—Babe Ruth? Ruth's dead! You've got good stuff. If you didn't, I wouldn't have brought you up. Quit being so careful. Go after the hitter. Get ahead in the count."

Although I was being aired out, I was sure that I heard a compliment hidden in Tommy's words. *I've got good stuff? He brought me to the big leagues because he believes in me?*

Tommy wasn't done. "If I could get a heart surgeon in here, I'd have him open my chest and take out my heart. Then I'd have him open your chest, take out your heart, and tell him to give you mine. With my heart and your arm, you'd be in the Hall of Fame! I've seen guys come and go, son, and you've got it."

Tommy finished his sermon with a flourish. "Take charge! Make 'em hit your best stuff! Be aggressive. Be a bulldog out there." And then, almost like he had surprised himself with a stroke of genius, he announced, "That's going to be your new name: Bulldog. It's the ninth inning, we bring you in and you're facing Dale Murphy. He hears, 'Now pitching, Orel Hershiser.' He can't wait till you get in there. But if he hears, 'Now pitching, *Bulldog* Hershiser,' he's thinking, *Oh, no, who's that?* Murphy's going to be scared to death!"

I admit that I was a little insulted by the rah-rah pep talk and the nickname, but I knew Tommy had spoken the truth. I had been tentative and too careful. Two days later we were in a tough situation against the San Francisco Giants. The call came from the dugout, "Can anybody down there pitch?" The bullpen was spent so I volunteered, in spite of a tender elbow and an arm weak from overwork.

I'll never forget the walk to the mound and the three innings that followed. I could hear Tommy shouting from the dugout, "C'mon, Bulldog! You can do it, Bulldog! You're my man,

Bulldog!" I was a major leaguer. I was good enough to be here and had what it took to win. And I started to believe it because it's what my skipper had told me.

Tommy Lasorda had introduced me to the importance of truth-telling—tactless as it was—and the power of an encouraging coach.

A TEACHABLE SPIRIT

You may be thinking, *All of this is interesting, but I'm not an athlete. I don't need a coach to help with my pitching or give me a clever nickname. How does all of this apply to me?*

That's a good question.

Remember my early coaches were people who helped me with life, not just baseball. My dad, who was never satisfied with average. My mom, who believed in her children. My Grandpa Gillman, who lived his life as a consummate gentleman and ready student. Dave Martin, who spoke well of others. Burt Hooton, who took time with a lowly rookie. And Tommy Lasorda, who spoke the truth.

> "Take charge! Make 'em hit your best stuff! Be aggressive. Be a bulldog out there."

My best coaches have not always been the ones who knew the game. Their best counsel has not always been about playing baseball. They've been people who set a standard for my life, giving me something to follow. So I've looked for coaches—experts—in finance, health and fitness, spiritual disciplines, parenting, business, and organizational skills. These people have helped to shape me.

Over the years, after a good outing, I have heard people compliment me on my baseball skills. I have watched the late night

But here's the headline I will always aspire to: "Orel Hershiser: A man with a teachable spirit."

edition of ESPN's *Sports-Center* or *Baseball Tonight* or read complimentary accounts in the paper the next morning.

Clever headlines over the years have been fun to see:

"Reds Fail Orel Exam!" after a big win against Cincinnati.

"OOO OOO OOOrel," during my record-breaking scoreless inning streak.

"Hot Dog," on the day when, in hundred-degree heat and with one day's rest, I beat the Expos at Shea Stadium.

"Dog Gone," when I retired from the game.

But here's the headline I will always aspire to: "Orel Hershiser: A man with a teachable spirit."

Who have your coaches been? What good things did they teach you? Be on the lookout for good coaches. Watch their lives, listen to their advice . . . and believe them. You may never achieve what you want to accomplish if you don't have someone in your life who has already found what you are striving for.

Even though I've retired from baseball, I'll never be too old for another coach to believe in.

PRINCIPLE #2

Anything Can Happen

In the summer of 1984, just a few weeks after Tommy Lasorda had dubbed me Bulldog, I walked into the visitor's clubhouse at Shea Stadium. Nothing had been unusual about the day so far. My ride to the ballpark on the team bus had been uneventful. The security folks and clubhouse guys had said their hellos in their usual way.

But as I rounded the corner from the clubhouse door and walked to the center of the large area where our lockers encircled the room, I saw something I will never forget. Even now I can clearly remember the next few seconds as though it happened yesterday.

In front of every locker was a small round stool that we used as we got dressed. Sitting on top of my stool was a baseball. My first thought was, *I wonder who left a baseball there? Maybe someone needs an autograph.*

Then it hit me. *This ball's for me. I'm pitching today—I'm starting!*

I glanced over my shoulder, looking toward the short hallway that led to Tommy's office. He was watching me, leaning up against the doorway, his arms folded across his chest. And he was smiling like a proud father, waiting for his son to open a present on Christmas morning.

"You got the ball today, Bulldog," he said in a voice loud enough for everyone in the clubhouse to hear. Never one to avoid an opportunity for the dramatic, Tommy didn't want my teammates to miss this moment either. A couple of guys came over and shook my hand; others called out their congratulations.

"Way to go, Bulldog!" someone called from the training room.

"Bury the Mets, Orel!" another said from his locker.

I walked over and picked up the ball. I turned it slowly in my hand, knowing that this was what I had dreamed about since my first visit to Tiger Stadium as a little kid. It was my first start in the big leagues. I felt myself filling with emotion but quickly pushed it back down. *Not now, Orel.* This wasn't the time or the place . . . but it was an awesome moment.

It was not unusual for a manager to keep a pitcher in the dark about his first start. Most skippers wanted to keep it from becoming too much of a big deal. First, they don't want to interrupt the player's workout routine or risk too much anticipation, sacrificing a good night's sleep. Secondly, they don't want the media to get wind of it, subjecting the pitcher to interviews and possibly getting him all hyped up about the start.

That day, Tommy had been forced to go to the bullpen for a starter, since Jerry Reuss and Rick Honeycutt had been injured. He decided to give me my first shot and fill the hole in the rotation.

Conventional baseball wisdom says that you never know when your break will come. Always be ready.

This was my time. I had the ball. Was I ready?

On May 26, 1984, I went to the mound against the New York Mets. The mighty New York Mets: Darryl Strawberry, George Foster, Keith Hernandez, and the rest of the team. I pitched six scoreless innings. I felt great. But in the bottom of the seventh, I gave up a home run to Hubie Brooks, then walked Ron Hodges on four pitches, and Tommy walked to the mound to pull me out of the game. "Good work, Bulldog," he said, taking the ball from my hand and swatting me on the butt. As I walked to the dugout, my teammates met me on the steps, congratulating me on what I had done.

Tommy brought in Tom "Buffalo Head" Niedenfuer from the bullpen. Tom was a solid closer with a great pick-off move to first. Sure enough, after a few pitches, Tom caught pinch runner Kelvin Chapman leaning toward second and snapped a quick throw to Greg Brock. Since Chapman had been my responsibility, I was off the hook.

Unfortunately for him, Niedenfuer gave up a run later in the inning and took the loss.

I remember Buffalo Head needling me in the clubhouse after the game. "I come in and pick off *your* guy," he chided, "but *my* guy scores and I get the loss. Thanks a lot, Bulldog."

> "You got the ball today, Bulldog," he said in a voice loud enough for everyone in the clubhouse to hear.

Although I didn't get the decision, I knew that I had done my job. I had come to the ballpark that morning, expecting a great day in the big leagues. But "You got the ball, Bulldog," made it unforgettable. Tommy had watched me prepare and he'd believed I was ready.

But being ready isn't just about life's pleasant surprises like that first start in 1984. Readiness is also about the inevitable painful things life has to offer.

SOMETHING'S WRONG

Spring Training in 1990 had been cut short because of a work stoppage. And it was during these few weeks in Vero Beach that I began to notice something was different about my shoulder.

Poking around at the muscles and bones of my shoulder and arm had always been a habit of mine. My family and friends will tell you that this was something I did a lot while sitting in a restaurant or watching TV. In my digging around I found a strange sensation in my shoulder. There was an instability that hadn't been there before—a softness, a hollowness. In my movements I would hear suction sounds. Pockets of air and fluid seemed to be filling these spaces.

While doing something ordinary like tucking in my shirt, I would feel my shoulder slip out of place. I knew something strange was going on, but I was sure that I could work it out. I knew I would be all right—nothing a little hard work wouldn't cure.

I just need to work harder, I said to myself. *All I need to do is get stronger.*

So I talked to Pat Screnar, the Dodger therapist. And I asked our team physician, Dr. Frank Jobe, for advice. In my questions, I tried to stay upbeat, hoping for comments like, "Oh, yeah, we went through this same thing with this other guy, we told him to do these things, and he was fine the next year."

I hoped for this, but it's not what I heard.

Instead, I could tell by the way Pat described things to me, the new exercises he would give me . . . even his mannerisms and expressions, that this was not routine. I kept working.

Spring training ended. Jamie, my two boys, and I flew from Vero Beach to Los Angeles for the beginning of the regular season. I was joined in the starting rotation by veterans Mike Morgan, Fernando Valenzuela, Tim Belcher, and a gifted young pitcher named Ramón Martinez.

Now that I was facing live action and games that mattered, the looseness in my shoulder began to ache. And soon the ache

> *I just need to work harder,* I said to myself. *All I need to do is get stronger.*

turned to pain—then to *sharp* pain. I continued to pitch.

The pain forced me to make adjustments on the mound. I could only throw my fastball every three or four pitches. The impact of throwing the ball ninety miles an hour would literally pull my arm out of its socket. Pain would shoot down from my shoulder to my fingertips. I tried to camouflage the grimaces that would expose me. I would "recover" by throwing a mix of slow curves, change-ups, or BP (batting practice) fastballs.

After throwing a few less punishing pitches, I'd feel some strength coming back into my shoulder. *Okay*, I'd think to myself, *now I need to throw a fastball again. I can do this.* I'd throw another ninety-mile-an-hour fastball, wince from the pain, and start the cycle again.

Between starts, my shoulder was in constant pain. I couldn't even pull my wallet out of my back pocket or reach around in the car to grab something off the backseat. But I was still in a serious case of denial. *They're paying me to pitch and I'll figure out a way to get it done.*

> The impact of throwing the ball ninety miles an hour would literally pull my arm out of its socket.

After four starts and an uncharacteristically high ERA of 4.26, I reluctantly decided to ask for help. I had done everything I could think of to avoid this moment but had run completely out of options. As I walked off the mound after getting bombed by St. Louis, I glanced into the stands where I knew Jamie was sitting. She squeezed out an encouraging and upbeat smile, but we both knew better.

It was an unusually cold day, so there were very few ballplayers' wives at the park. Jamie had braved the weather to support me, but even my stalwart wife couldn't stand it. Later she told me that while I was pitching, she had stood and shouted, "Get him out of there!"

Uncharacteristic doesn't begin to describe Jamie's outburst. Who could blame her? She knew I was in serious trouble.

Dr. Jobe scheduled me for an MRI the next day at the Kerlan-Jobe Clinic. MRI normally stands for Magnetic Resonance Imaging, but during some of my more creative moments, I renamed the machine "Maybe Really Injured" or "Might Require Incision."

As I got dressed that next morning for the drive to the clinic, I remember trying to sort all of this out. Ever the optimist, I quietly rationalized that I'd probably be on the DL (disabled list) for thirty days, sixty at the most. *Other pitchers have gone under the knife and come back quickly. I can get through this,* I rationalized.

Arthroscopic knee surgery after the 1987 season hadn't been a big deal. I was back to normal in no time. This time it wouldn't be any different.

An emergency appendectomy just one week before Spring Training in 1988 hadn't stopped me either. My surgeon, Dr. Jeff Hyde, had told me that I should be "up and around in three or four weeks." I'd decided I wasn't going to let a little thing like that keep me from getting to Spring Training on time. So I didn't pitch batting practice the first day . . . but I threw the second day and never looked back. I was confident that I could beat this shoulder problem the same way.

On the way to the clinic, Jamie and I were pretty quiet. What I did say came out with a hint of courage. Jamie didn't challenge me on my confidence. I knew she was hoping for the best, too.

We walked into the outpatient waiting area. Jamie was holding my hand. Unlike most of the times when you go for testing or minor surgery and are forced to stand in lines and fill out pages of forms, two nurses were actually waiting for us. They greeted us and led us directly to the elevators. I guess that being a Dodger had its privileges.

As we walked through crowded lobbies and past doctors and nurses in the halls, I was recognized. People smiled. Some of them called me by name. Of course, I was flattered by this attention, but I was clearly focused on something else. I wanted to know what was wrong with my arm and get back to pitching as soon as possible. Of course, I didn't breathe any of this to Jamie.

> *Other pitchers have gone under the knife and come back quickly. I can get through this, I rationalized.*

"I'M SORRY, OREL"

I closed my eyes and tried to relax. If you've ever been inside the tube of an MRI, you know how confining it is. But like a good coach, this machine was going to tell me the truth about my shoulder. And once I had that information, the doctors and I could put together the plan to get back on the mound again.

I can also remember being fascinated with what was happening at this moment. Like Grandpa Gillman leaning over the fender of his car in the shop and asking the mechanic endless questions, my mind was filled with speculation. But soon the rhythmic clicking sound began clearing my conscious thoughts. Standing on the other side of the glass, Jamie could tell by my methodic breathing on the intercom that I had fallen asleep. Between pitching the night before and the uncertainty of the past few days, exhaustion had overtaken my energetic mind. Just before falling off, I remember praying one more time.

Of course, the clinicians do not have permission to give any analysis, but once I had been removed from the MRI and was standing in front of their computer screens, I bombarded them with questions. "What's that?" I said, pointing to something on the screen. "And what's that? Does that look good to you? Does that look okay?"

No, this won't be too bad. It's just another challenge—another hill to climb.

The technicians smiled at me. "The doctors read these best," they joked. No one would answer any of my questions.

An aide led us up two floors to Dr. Jobe's empty office. Jamie and I sat down in the two chairs facing his desk. I avoided the temptation to poke around at my shoulder. I knew that it was too late for that so I folded my hands.

We sat quietly, looking around at the framed documents on his walls. On the wall to our left were the X ray light boxes that I figured would soon tell the story. We didn't talk. Dread was beginning to gain some ground in the pit of my stomach, but I said nothing about it.

In a few minutes, Dr. Jobe walked in. It was reassuring to see him. Even though his face was unusually somber, it felt good to have him there. I stood to greet him but did not offer my hand. Reaching across a desk to shake hands would have been too painful. Instead I smiled and we both sat down.

Almost as though it had been scripted, at that moment Dr. Ralph Gambardella walked in, carrying several large X rays. He handed them to Dr. Jobe, turned, and walked out. Taking the X rays, Dr. Jobe stood and snapped two of them into the light box. He returned to his desk and sat down.

He looked straight at me and said, "I'm sorry, Orel. I'm afraid this is very serious."

I slowly nodded, my eyes filling with tears. I didn't try to hold them back. In this moment, that would have been a useless effort. Jamie reached over and took my hand.

Dr. Jobe explained how years of pitching had taken their toll on my shoulder. He leaned forward. "You've been pitching in a lot of pain haven't you, Orel?"

"I'm sorry, Orel. I'm afraid this is very serious."

"Yeah, I have," I answered, smiling at the thought that I finally could tell this man the absolute truth.

Dr. Jobe paused, then continued. "You've been pitching in *tremendous* pain."

The smile cleared from my face. I nodded.

I can remember his professionalism as he spoke. But I can also remember his kindness, his tenderness, and his genuine caring. Dr. Jobe knew what this meant. Even though he didn't say it, I knew I was in trouble.

"We'll start by scoping your shoulder, but I think you may need some reconstruction." Then he added, "If you want to get a second opinion, I'll certainly understand."

I was taken aback by his humility and immediately assured him that I had no interest in going anywhere else. We scheduled surgery for the next morning.

On the drive back from Englewood, Jamie and I said very little. I flipped on the radio. Michael Bolton's voice penetrated the silence.

Gonna break these chains around me
Gonna learn to fly again
May be hard, may be hard
But I'll do it
When I'm back on my feet again
Soon these tears will all be dryin'
Soon these eyes will see the sun
Might take time, might take time
But I'll see it
When I'm back on my feet again
When I'm back on my feet again
I'll walk proud down this street again
And they'll all look at me again

And they'll see that I'm strong
Gonna hear the children laughing
Gonna hear the voices sing
Won't be long, won't be long
Till I hear them
When I'm back on my feet again
Gonna feel the sweet light of heaven
Shining down its light on me
One sweet day, one sweet day
I will feel it
When I'm back on my feet again
And I'm not gonna crawl again
I will learn to stand tall again
No I'm not gonna fall again
Cos I'll learn to be strong
Soon these tears will all be dryin'
Soon these eyes will see the sun
Won't be long, won't be long
Till I see it
When I'm back on my feet again
When I'm back on my feet again
I'll be back on my feet again

Tears streamed down my face. I was filled with a strange combination of anxiety and determination. This would be my anthem. I *would* get back on my feet again.

We drove to our home. In just a few minutes, John Werhas, our chapel leader, was there. I told him of Dr. Jobe's prognosis. Soon other friends joined us. We talked, read from the Bible, and prayed together.

Jamie and I drove to Dodger Stadium. Word had traveled quickly that I was headed for season-ending surgery. A press conference was called and I faced cameras and microphones. Near the start of the conference a reporter asked how I felt, facing surgery less than two years after reaching the pinnacle of my career. Most of the conference was a blur, but my answer to that one reporter summed up what was in my heart.

"The God who was with me in 1988 is the same God who is with me right now."

> Tears streamed down my face. I was filled with a strange combination of anxiety and determination.

Even though I was afraid, I was comforted by this fact.

Jamie and I drove back to our home. Jamie stayed with the boys while my friend Jim Rhodes drove me to the hospital. I was admitted to a private room where I was presented with some interesting forms to sign. I didn't read the fine print, but it might as well have read:

RELEASE

If my arm falls off during surgery, I promise not to sue the hospital.

And I will still provide plenty of signed baseballs for the fund-raiser auction.

If I die, I will still find a way to provide lots of free Dodger tickets to all the hospital administrators and their sons and daughters.

Signed,
Orel Hershiser IV

If you've had surgery, you remember signing these "release" forms, don't you?

Several close friends came by the hospital to wish me well. Before they left, they circled my bed and prayed for wisdom for Dr. Jobe and healing for me. They also prayed for Jamie and the boys.

After a long and fitful night of semisleep, I was happy to see the sun peek through my hospital room. *Let's get on with this*, I remember thinking to myself, once I had gotten my bearings and remembered what day this was. I could hear nurses hustling up and down the hallway outside, their shoes squeaking on the polished floor. The intercom gave out a constant chatter, calling doctors and asking them to dial number so-and-so.

In a few minutes, Jamie appeared in the doorway. It was good to see her.

"Good morning, Honey," she said, her voice filled with reassurance. God had certainly answered our friends' prayers. Her confidence and calm spirit seemed to fill the room. She reached down and hugged me, then sat next to the bed, and we talked for a few minutes. A nurse interrupted our conversation with a syringe filled with something to lighten my head.

Drowsiness was almost immediate. And with my fading inhibitions came a deepening panic. Seeing this, Jamie picked up my Bible and began reading from the Psalms. Soon she climbed into my bed and held me. I remember crying—first the sniffling kind, then sobs from somewhere deep inside.

"Don't let them do this," I wept. "I can still pitch. I can still pitch."

A couple of attendants entered my room. They slid me onto a gurney, wheeling me out of my room and down the hall. As Jamie walked beside the gurney, Robert Fraley, my attorney, sport's representative, and best friend, joined her. The attendants pushed me onto one of those huge elevators. As the elevator descended, I called out, "Don't let them do this. Please don't let them do this. I don't want this surgery. I don't want this."

Jamie and Robert stood on either side, holding my hands. I don't remember anything else.

WHILE I WAS SLEEPING

During rehab I had a lot of hopeless days, especially when there was a setback or when I felt like I wasn't making any progress.

On most of those days, I would crawl in bed at night feeling like the surgery hadn't worked. It was on these days that I had to trust the men who knew more than I did about my situation, rather than my own feelings.

I've talked about believing and trusting good coaches. Putting my faith in Pat Screnar and Dr. Jobe was just another opportunity for the same, except that these guys weren't just giving me advice on baseball mechanics or good manners; they were literally making calls that would determine the future of my career.

But they weren't guessing—they were prepared for this. Both of these men had actually seen inside my shoulder. They had tinkered with the bones, ligaments, and tendons that held it together. Yes, I said *both* of them.

> I remember crying—first the sniffling kind, then sobs from somewhere deep inside. "Don't let them do this," I wept. "I can still pitch. I can still pitch."

Pat Screnar was a physical therapist—one of baseball's best. But he was not a doctor. The morning of the surgery, Dr. Jobe announced to his team of physicians and attending nurses that Pat was going to join them in the operating room. And whatever their surprise must have been at that news, it wouldn't have compared to their shock when Dr. Jobe put Pat on the seat of honor—the place with the best view, directly across from him—as he did his work inside my shoulder.

Here was one of the world's premier surgeons, performing experimental surgery on one of America's most visible sports figures. This was the hottest ticket in town.

Six years before the surgery, during my first few days as a Dodger, Pat had put me through a battery of tests. Using a goniometer, he and his assistant measured my internal and external range of motion. They calibrated my flexibility and the exact angle of my arm when it was retracted and extended.

I remember being fascinated with what Pat was doing. "Why are you doing all of this?" I joked. "I'm a baseball player, not an astronaut." Pat patiently answered all my questions. Some guys dreaded all this technical rigmarole. I was completely captivated by it.

Each of Pat's measurements had been carefully recorded and saved. Now, as Dr. Jobe prepared to take my shoulder apart and put it back together, he asked Pat to join him. In fact, Pat brought those original measurements and the goniometer with him into the operating room so they could make the adjustments that matched my shoulder in its prime. Throughout this surgery, they were returning my shoulder to its God-given measurements.

Once the incision had been made into my shoulder and the muscle had been carefully retracted, it became clear what the problem was. "This looks like pounded veal in here," Dr. Jobe exclaimed once he had a good look. (Pat told me this later. Thankfully, I didn't hear it myself.)

Like a hammer, the humeral head of my upper arm had destroyed everything in its path. I hadn't needed surgery, Dr. Jobe told me several days later. I'd needed radical shoulder reconstruction. Even though I had been around big-league trainers and physicians, I had not heard those words before.

Dr. Jobe carefully cleaned out all the "shrapnel" and began his work. Following a procedure, it was Dr. Jobe's practice to describe exactly what he had done to his patients, in layman's terms. This is how I remember his explanation to me.

Because the shoulder is capable of multiple rotating movements, it is quite different than other joints. The shoulder is more like a golf ball sitting on top of a golf tee. The rim of the tee (the glenoid labrum) keeps the head of the upper arm (humerus) in place. It's held in place by tendons and ligaments.

A sturdy balloonlike membrane surrounds all of this, called the shoulder capsule.

From years of throwing, the front of my golf tee (anterior labrum) had been completely destroyed, allowing my arm to fall off the tee each time I threw the ball. This stretched the ligaments, allowing the bone to pound into the delicate capsule tissue.

> "This looks like pounded veal in here," Dr. Jobe exclaimed once he had a good look.

Dr. Jobe had carefully separated the muscle fibers, clearing out the bits of bone and tissue in his way. He had then drilled three holes into what used to be my anterior labrum, attaching three steel anchors to help him construct a new front for my shoulder.

"Is that tight enough?" Dr. Jobe had asked Pat as he pulled on the sutures attached to the anchors.

Pat lifted my arm and checked his instruments. "Since his problem is instability, let's make him a little tight," he responded. "I can break it loose if I have to. I can always stand on it," he jokingly added.

"Good, then let's pull it tighter." (At this moment, general anesthesia was my closest friend.)

On his way out of my shoulder, after reattaching everything, Dr. Jobe had overlapped the portion of the capsule that had been stretched out, making it twice as resilient as it was before. Not only was my shoulder as good as new, it had the potential of being *better* than new . . . although no professional thrower had ever completely recovered from anything like this before.

SCAR TISSUE

My first few days at home were very difficult. My arm spent most of the time in a huge brace that held it out from my body,

Not only was my shoulder as good as new, it had the potential of being *better* than new.

like it was resting on a shelf. *This has to go ninety miles an hour and get big-league hitters out,* I'd think to myself. *Yeah . . . sure.*

I remember looking at myself in the mirror. It was surreal, almost as though I were seeing someone else standing there, someone who certainly could never be an athlete again. I fought depression.

Not since running away from BG had I been at this kind of rock bottom. But, unlike then, I was not here because of my poor choices. So, although it may sound like a cliché, for the first time in my life I was dependent on my faith, my family, and my friends. There were times of prayer alone, thanking God for his love and pleading with Him for his mercy. There were moments when Jamie would sit next to me on the couch and hold me. Words were unavailable and unnecessary. Even at the tender age of six, my son Quinton did his best to encourage me. We'd lay on the floor and play games or sit and cuddle on the couch, watching his videos.

There were friends like Jim and Susie Rhodes and Dave and Jan Hotchkin who dropped everything to be with us. They brought food, words of comfort, laughter, and nonstop prayer. I don't know what I would have done without them.

Robert Fraley had jumped on a red-eye from New York to be with me the morning of the surgery. His presence and the encouraging words from his wife, Dixie, meant more to me than I could ever have expressed at the time. Even now I'm amazed when I think of their consistent caring and support.

And don't think that my dad would have missed this. He was standing there in my hospital room as I woke from the anesthesia. Mom would have come, but she had to stay at home to be near my grandmother.

But in spite of all this love and care, the hard work of rehabilitation was on—pardon the expression—my *own* shoulders. I was the first big leaguer to have this surgery. No one really expected me to ever retake the mound in a major-league game.

That's what they said. I had other plans.

My first rehab assignment was to take my arm out of the brace and stand in the hot shower with the water beating on me. I put my hand on the tile and walked my fingers upward as far as I could go, moving my chest closer and closer to the wall. Trying each day to improve my mobility, I would mark how high I would get before the pain and stiffness stopped me. I did this three times a day.

I would also lay on my back on the family room floor, lifting my arm as far as I could, holding it for ten or fifteen seconds. "Just past the point of pain," Pat Screnar had told me. Although I remember wondering if I was doing too much too soon, I trusted Pat and Dr. Jobe.

What they told me at the time was that these early exercises and movements were shaping the scar tissue inside my shoulder into something helpful—something good. During surgery Dr. Jobe had allowed for some isolated internal bleeding in precise places to make sure that scar tissue would form. Now I was taking the head of the bone in my upper arm and literally using it like sandpaper to grind a new front rim on my golf tee.

Under the care of consummate professionals, this scar tissue—a potential adversary—was becoming my friend.

MY VERY OWN MEMORIAL DAY

On May 29, 1991, two days before America's official Memorial Day, I walked to the mound in Dodger Stadium for what would be a memorable day for me. Just over one year after the surgery, I did what no one had ever done: returned to the big leagues after major shoulder reconstruction. Even long-time beat reporters would call it "a miracle."

I had pictured this day during endless hours of rehab and now it was really happening. It was an awesome moment.

After quickly gathering my composure, I wound up and threw my first warm-up pitch. I could hear the pop of my fastball burying itself in the soft leather of Mike Scioscia's mitt. The sound was loud and wonderfully familiar.

> No one really expected me to ever retake the mound in a major-league game. That's what they said. I had other plans.

Glancing into the stands, Jamie and I caught each other's eye. Mine filled with tears. I knew hers did, too. Even though these were just practice throws, I knew that all the work was worth it.

Because I was truly grateful for Dr. Frank Jobe and Pat Screnar's help in bringing me to this moment, I had written a letter to each one with the instructions, "Please open and read before I throw my first post-op pitch."

Getting ready wasn't something I had done alone. I wouldn't have been here without these men.

Even though I knew I had a long way to go, as a bonus something wonderful happened that day. We were playing against the Houston Astros. The lead-off man was Steve Finley, a left-handed hitter. My very first pitch to him was low and away and Finley chipped a foul ball directly over the third base dugout.

My good friend Harry Scolinos was there in the stands, surrounded by hundreds of fans who would have loved to snatch a foul ball. Finley's foul sailed directly into Harry's hands. He told me later that he didn't have to move at all. Several days later Harry presented me with the ball, mounted on a stand with a small engraved plaque.

Orel Returns

May 29, 1991

For nothing is impossible with God.

Luke 1:37

Among my trophies and awards, this is still one of my most prized possessions.

After my first post-op win, Jamie and I invited Dr. Jobe and Pat Screnar and their wives, Robert and Dixie Fraley, and my parents, along with lots of our closest friends, to a special celebration dinner.

After presenting Dr. Jobe and Pat with trophies I'd had specially designed for them, I used the example of water—H_20—being two parts hydrogen and one part oxygen.

"It doesn't make any difference how these elements are held together or how all of this really works," I said. "It just does. Which of the three elements is the most important? Who knows? The point is that to make water you need all three. And together, the three of us have done something that doesn't need explanation. No one of the three of us was more important than the other . . . doctor, therapist, or patient. The fact is that we each did our job, it has worked, and that's enough."

> Getting ready wasn't something I'd had to do alone. I wouldn't have been here without these men.

Over the previous thirteen months, I had discovered that anything could happen. I had learned that making it through had not only required my own diligence but a commitment to the expertise of those in whom I had put my trust.

Seven and a half years after returning from surgery to the

mound, I was faced with another unbelievable challenge—something I couldn't have possibly anticipated.

OCTOBER 25, 1999

As you know, I have been so fortunate to have people in my life who were great examples of character, discipline, and readiness from the time I was a small boy—mentors who not only instructed me in how to be prepared, but men who lived it. There was Orel III—my dad—Grandpa Gillman, my coaches, managers, and my brilliant doctors and trainers.

And there was Robert Fraley.

October 21, 1999, Jamie and I loaded our car in New York and headed home. We (the Mets) had lost a bitter National League Championship Series (NLCS) battle with the Braves and I was starting another off-season. I hated losing such a hard-fought series, but I loved going home.

Our cell phone rang repeatedly as we drove south through the Carolinas and Georgia. As my friend and representative (he didn't like to be called an agent), Robert kept tabs on us as we made our way down the East Coast. "Where *are* you guys?" he'd laugh when I'd pick up my ringing phone. He never identified himself. He didn't need to. Throughout my career, his voice had become familiar and loved—always a pleasant surprise. I was more than just one of Robert Fraley's clients. I was his friend and I knew it.

I had suggested to Robert that we have lunch on Monday, the day after Jamie and I got home, to talk over several options for the next season. He had told me he was taking a quick trip to Dallas with our mutual friend, Payne Stewart. We tentatively scheduled something later in the week.

So on Monday Jamie and I went to lunch alone. It was great being back in familiar surroundings enjoying a relaxed time together. We finished lunch and went to pick up a few things at a

I was more than just one of Robert Fraley's clients. I was his friend and I knew it.

local specialty shop not far from our house. This was—and still is—one of our favorite places. I was joking with "Fish," the store's affable owner, when the store's phone rang. "Mr. Hershiser, it's for you," one of the clerks said, handing me the telephone.

I quickly glanced at my cell phone, wondering why the call hadn't come through the usual way. I immediately got the answer—I could see there was no reception.

"Orel, this is Gordie." It was my brother. "Find Dixie. Robert's plane is in trouble," he said, his voice filled with tremendous urgency.

"What's the matter?" I asked.

"They can't communicate with anyone on Robert's plane. It's flying on autopilot."

I yelled to Jamie, who was upstairs in the store. "JAMIE! WE HAVE TO GO. WE NEED TO GO *RIGHT NOW*."

Hearing my raised voice and stern tone, she hurried down the stairs. As we dashed to the parking lot, I filled her in on what I had heard. We jumped into the car and sped toward Tracey Stewart's house while I called Dixie Fraley, who had just received a call from Cindy Lisk, Robert's assistant. Then I called my friend, Robert Wolgemuth, told him the news, and asked him to pray.

In a few minutes we were pulling up to Payne and Tracey Stewart's house. As we got out of the car, Gloria Baker, Payne's assistant, drove in with Chelsea and Aaron, Payne and Tracey's children. The next few minutes were filled with indescribable tears of pain and disbelief. I promised Tracey that I would keep in constant contact with her but that I needed to get to Dixie's house immediately.

By the time we arrived at Robert and Dixie's home, the television reports had confirmed the plane's final plummet to the ground in North Dakota, a thousand miles from its intended destination.

"We need to pray for the medical personnel on the ground to help the people on the plane," Dixie pleaded.

"Oh, Dixie," I remember saying. "There's no one to help. No one survived."

Jamie and I held Dixie, just as she and Robert had held us during my rehab eight years before. Dixie's soul mate and two close friends were gone.

During the afternoon, I spent time in Robert's home office. I looked on the bookshelf and saw the gift I had given him following the '88 season. It was a large ship's compass with the inscription, "Thanks for your guidance."

Since my first meeting with Robert Fraley in Vero Beach in 1984, Robert had been my go-to guy. He had provided stability and wisdom and godly advice. Now it was my turn. Over the next few days, Jamie and I served Dixie in every way we could. The phone calls, deliveries of flowers, and parade of visitors was almost endless. During moments of calm, I walked around Robert's office.

I paused at his "standing desk" where he had his morning Bible reading and prayer. I walked over to the overstuffed leather chair where he read the morning paper. I circled his desk where he made his calls and saw several call-back reminder notes.

> "Oh, Dixie," I remember saying. "There's no one to help. No one survived."

He had had no idea that just a few hours before this moment, as he put a few things in his briefcase for the flight to Dallas, it would be his last morning there. The orderliness of his office gripped me. The quiet discipline of this man overwhelmed me. *Robert Fraley was ready*. I found myself saying these words over and over again to myself during the days that followed. And although he never wrote a book, Robert's story had been indelibly written on the hearts of hundreds of his friends and clients—especially on me.

The quiet discipline of this man overwhelmed me. *Robert Fraley was ready.*

On Thursday, just one week after Jamie and I had left New York for the off-season, I stood in front of hundreds of grieving friends and well-wishers and spoke these words:

On Monday afternoon, the day Robert died, Jamie and I raced to Dixie's. Sitting at Robert's desk, I saw why he was so prepared for anything—and so wise. To my left was a leadership study and a copy of *God's Little Instruction Book*. There was a marker in the book. The page read:

Leadership is a potent combination of strategy and character. But if you must be without one, be without strategy.

To my right were financial studies from some of the best minds in the world. On the shelf directly behind me was his well-worn Bible.

I walked to the room where Robert worked out. Above the door was this quote from St. Augustine:

Care for your body as though you were going to live forever. Care for your soul as if you were going to die tomorrow.

When a player asked me, "Who's your agent?" I would say, "I don't have an agent; I have a friend. He's a believer who's an attorney. He lives in Orlando, Florida. You probably don't know him. His name is Robert Fraley. F-R-A-L-E-Y." They'd ask, "Do you like him?" And I'd say, "We have a deal. Either I'll speak at his funeral or he'll speak at mine."

> *Leadership is a potent combination of strategy and character. But if you must be without one, be without strategy.*

Sometimes Robert and I would go for weeks without any contact. He's only been gone for three days and I miss him already.

From the example of Robert's life, I wanted to keep learning to be ready . . . because anything *can* happen.

YES, ANYTHING CAN HAPPEN

Nothing alters our lives like the unexpected—good things as well as failure and tragedy.

Even though it's what I had dreamed of and worked hard for, one of the ironies of playing baseball in the big leagues was that all my successes and failures were broadcast in brutal detail. Of course, it was fun to see the replay of things like my striking out Tony Phillips on a sinking fastball, sealing the final game of the '88 World Series. But over the years, in front of millions of television fans, I have been subjected to intricate slow-motion replays of my mistakes, too. And, if that were not enough, these mistakes have been examined for the vast viewing audience by sportscasters, gracing us with their "expert analysis."

Actually, all of this has been good for me.

Surviving life's good and bad in the public eye has taught me about being ready. Because of this I have been forced to learn that anything can happen. I'm glad for it.

I need to keep listening to the advice of coaches and experts, watching the lives of people I respect, and working as hard as I can.

And I want to keep learning how to be ready for anything—the wins *and* the losses. Maybe my experiences can be an encouragement for you to do the same.

PRINCIPLE #3

Sell Out to the Process

I was a late bloomer.

At most stages of my life, it's seemed like my peers were always physically and socially more mature than I was. That meant that from grade school all the way through my sophomore year in college, I had to hustle just to keep up. This was also true the first time I stepped onto a baseball diamond.

Looking back, I can see that my situation had its benefits. Having to work hard to keep up and compete was going to become a way of life. I understood that if I wanted to be successful in this game, I would have to do more than the other guys.

Regardless of my size, I knew that I had some natural athletic ability. As an eight-year-old, I won the Mid-East Personna "Throw, Hit, and Run" (like Ford Motor Company's "Punt, Pass & Kick") competition. This earned me a trip to New York and the national finals at Yankee Stadium, where I finished in third place.

For a kid who loved baseball like I did, you can imagine how it felt to walk onto the field at the world's most famous baseball stadium. *Wow, I want to come back here as a player some day,* I remember thinking.

But don't be fooled by my success. Everything about me was way behind the other kids. At least, that's how it felt.

PUTTING MY MIND TO IT

In spite of my slowly developing physique, I worked hard enough in Little League to keep up with the boys on the field. And in a few years, I passed them. By the time I was twelve, I made the all-star team. Walking to the batter's box for my last Little League at bat (AB), I thought it would be great to hit a home run. *This is your last time up in Little League. You might as well go out in style.* Even at twelve, I was beginning to understand the mental part of the game. (Yeah, right. Ha, ha.)

I can still see my line drive disappearing over the left field fence as I rounded first base. I had started Little League as an underdog and had finished with a dinger. (Ironically, with 810 ABs in the big leagues, this feat eluded me. Even though I hit over .200 as a major leaguer—a respectable batting average for a pitcher—I never hit a home run.)

If you had seen me as a twelve-year-old, I would not have impressed you with my body, speed, or power. So graduating to the next level of baseball brought on the same challenge I had faced as an eight-year-old. I was on the field with young men who were bigger, faster, stronger, and more mature than me. So I kept working. And by the time I was ready for high school, I was competing at a high level again.

Everything about me was way behind the other kids. At least, that's how it felt.

High school baseball started the cycle all over again.

As a freshman, I did everything I could to make the varsity team. But I didn't. I'll never forget standing in front of Coach

Martin's office, reading the posted list of guys who had just made the varsity team. Some of my friends were on the list. But I didn't see my name. I scanned it again. No "Orel Hershiser." My heart sank. But I went back to work.

Although it was only the freshman team, I focused everything I had on being successful. When the coach told us to run ten laps, I stayed on the field and ran twelve. When he told us that practice was at four o'clock, I'd be there by three-thirty. I did not do this to impress my coach. I did it for myself . . . well, maybe a *little* to get noticed.

A year later, I stood in the same spot in front of Coach Martin's office, looking and hoping. More of my friends had made the team, but again, my name was not there. I was crushed; but I went back to work. This time I was determined to be the best player on the JV team. I was getting closer but wasn't there yet.

The summer after my sophomore year, I pumped gas at the Exxon station on the corner of Kresson Road and Route 70 in Cherry Hill. The station was close enough to our house that my parents could run me to the corner for work—since I didn't have a car. I loved having a job that gave me a chance to meet people. It was fun working in a place where I also saw lots of folks I knew.

But the best part was the check every two weeks. This was my first paying job and although I only made $3.50 an hour, it felt great to be making money on my own. With a steady income I started to dream about financial success. Believe it or not, late one night, I remember sitting on my bed, doing the math. *If I work hard and can get to ten dollars an hour and work for fifty years, I'll be a millionaire!* I never considered rent, car payments, or a little thing like taxes that I might run into along the way. But, for now, that didn't matter.

Finally, as a junior I made the team and was a pretty good player. But the next year, as a senior, I had an outstanding season. So much so that I was recognized by a few colleges and made the All-South Jersey team. Just like every time before, I had started the process as low man on the totem pole and had finished near the top.

At Bowling Green, the experience was identical. As a freshman I didn't make the team, even though I had a partial scholarship. As a sophomore, I thought that *this* would be the year. But, again, I didn't make it. But the summer after my sophomore year, something amazing happened.

I got a job at the printing company in Livonia, Michigan, where my dad was one of the owners. It was hard, manual labor and I put in as much time as I could. What happened during that summer was that my late-blooming body decided to cut loose. Working the late shift, I'd go early in the afternoon. My mom would pack me five sandwiches along with plenty of chips. By dinnertime I was starving. Consistent with her kind and unselfish ways, sometimes in the early evening she'd bring me a full dinner plate covered with foil and I'd practically inhale it. When I'd get home just before midnight, I'd go to the refrigerator and eat again!

> I did not do this to impress my coach. I did it for myself.

I remember my mother kiddingly saying many times as I headed out to work, "We can't keep you in jeans. Those pants are too short already!"

When fall rolled around and I was ready to go back to BG for my junior year, I had gained twenty pounds and grown three inches in two and a half months. Walking onto the practice field, everyone saw the change. I not only thought I could play at a higher level, but now I looked like I could play. It felt great. Best of all, I made the varsity team. I didn't even have to go look at the posted list. I knew I had made it from conversations with Coach Pervis and my teammates.

And, not only did I make the team, but by the end of my junior year I made enough of an impact that I started opening up some eyes, including getting the attention of some pro scouts.

> I not only thought I could play at a higher level, but now I looked like I could play.

When I was drafted by the Dodgers, it was a dream come true. I was actually going to become a pro baseball player (although being drafted in the seventeenth round made me more of a suspect than a prospect). That first Spring Training, I looked around at guys on the field who had been picked in the first and second round. They had been more successful than me, but I had been down this road before. All I knew was that I was being given a chance and I needed to give it my best shot.

VERY NEAR THE TOP

In looking back over my career and life, I've noted the people, experiences, and ideas that shaped me. These things—we settled on calling them *principles*—are the reason this book was born. Each of these principles has been important for me, but if someone twisted my arm and forced me to rank them in order of importance, this one would be right up there, very close to the top. It's a principle I discovered after years of cycling through the struggle of achievement at every level: "Sell out to the process."

It has been one of the most powerful driving forces in my life.

Please don't get the wrong idea here. *Sell out* does not mean *selling out,* like compromising or giving up. *Sell out* means complete commitment, surrender—just doing it. And the target of that resolution may surprise you.

The principle is not "Sell out to the results." It's not "Sell out to winning" or even "Sell out to success." It's "Sell out to the process."

Here's what I mean.

There were times during my career when I would be upset after a good outing and other times when I was fine, even upbeat, after I had gotten poor results. The principle of selling out to the process was at work. My dejection after a win could have come from my knowing that the win had come *in spite of* my performance.

During a crucial moment in the game, I had laid a fastball over the middle of the plate, right in a hitter's wheelhouse. Instead of blasting it 350 feet, like he should have, he popped it up to the shortstop. I knew the hitter well enough to know that if I did that again, he'd hit it out. Regardless of the result—which in this case had been good for me—I knew success had not come from my good work but from the hitter's failure to deliver. Maybe a hitter was able to make solid contact with my pitches, but his line drives were hit directly at my teammates. Or he exercised poor discipline, chasing pitches that got away from me.

> But if someone twisted my arm and forced me to rank them in order of importance, this one would be right up there, very close to the top.

Did I get the win? Yes. But was there complete concentration? No. Leading up to the game and during my performance I knew that I had allowed for lapses in preparation, focus, and concentration. There was no reason to celebrate.

And there were times when I had my best stuff. My regimen before the outing was satisfactory. My mechanics, my rhythm, the velocity and movement of the ball during the game were everything I had prepared for. But whatever good I was doing on the mound, the guys in the batter's box were having better fortune. Ground balls trickled through holes in the infield and bloopers dropped barely out of my teammates' reach.

As highly talented opponents, they were just doing their job.

So, in spite of how well I was doing, batters hit my best stuff and I took the loss. This did not upset me.

Don't misunderstand. I'm a competitor. I always preferred winning over losing. But I knew that when I won without deserving it or earning it, I couldn't rely on the consistency of that outcome. I was counting on pure luck or my opponent's mistakes to compensate for my lack of sound execution.

And if I lost, even though I was performing at a reasonable level, I knew that the "law of baseball probabilities" would turn my way and I would eventually win . . . and win more often than lose.

SOME APPLICATIONS OF THIS PRINCIPLE

Before going on, let me show you what this principle looks like in the world outside of baseball—the world where you might live.

Let's say that a salesman goes in to a potential customer. The salesman is not ready for this meeting. He hasn't taken time to study the benefits of his own product, he doesn't understand the needs of his customer, and he feels terrible. The night before he stayed out too late and drank too much. His head is throbbing.

He shows up for his appointment a few minutes late, but close enough for him. His customer is waiting and, although he shows the salesman some mercy, he's a little annoyed by the salesman's lack of punctuality.

Halfway through a poor presentation, the buyer stops the meeting. "I'll buy a freight car full of what you're selling." The salesman is ecstatic and, frankly, shocked at how easy that was. As he heads for door he calls his office on his cell phone and tells his assistant to cancel the rest of his appointments for the day. "I'm headed for the country club," he says. Getting into his car

> I was counting on pure luck or my opponent's mistakes to compensate for my lack of sound execution.

he smiles to himself, amazed at his ability to land the big order. "This is too easy," he says out loud as pulls his car out of the parking lot.

Actually, he was right. It was too easy. What the salesman knew but was not admitting was that his customer had been sold before the meeting. The buyer was out of the product and desperately needed some. Right now. Neither the quality of the presentation nor the skill of the salesman had landed the sale.

The salesman had won, but he had won in spite of his preparation, not because of it. If he continued to count on future success based on this performance, he was headed for failure.

For the salesman, selling out to the process would have meant that being ready for the presentation would have been more important than landing the order. As long as he continued to study the benefits of his product and the needs of his customers, "the law of sales probabilities" would eventually catch up to him. He would be successful.

What about a student who sits down to take a test and by pure luck guesses correctly on the questions and does well? Instead of preparing, she had sloughed off. Unfortunately, her reward for laziness is a passing grade. "This is easy," she says to herself. So the next time she faces a test she decides—hopes—that she'll guess well again. She doesn't do the hard work of preparation.

The student may get lucky again and pass the test. Or maybe not.

An understanding of selling out to the process might not have changed the results of the salesman's call or the student's test, but it would have given them the tools they needed to repeat their successes.

I had been in the big leagues less than two years when the power of this concept changed everything.

ONE DAY AT WRIGLEY FIELD

The highlight film of my career includes the fly ball I got Keith Moreland to hit to José Gonzalez in San Diego, giving me fifty-nine consecutive scoreless innings and breaking Don Drysdale's "unbreakable" record. The highlight reel also includes some of the great moments from the '88 play-offs. There are some clips of my first start after shoulder reconstruction in 1991 and my time in the post-season with Los Angeles, Cleveland, and New York. And there is a shot of me reaching a career total of two hundred wins during the summer of 1999.

This was when the idea of "Sell out to the process" really took hold.

But, for me, one of the greatest events in my career came in a hectic post-game moment in the visitor's clubhouse at Wrigley Field. Although I had been practicing it for a long time, this was when the idea of "Sell out to the process" really took hold. In my journey to the big leagues, I had tried to live out the principle. But in this moment, my thought processes went to the next subtle—but very important—level.

During the summer of 1984, my first full year in the majors, I pitched a two-hit shutout against the Cubs. The wind was so strong that the pennants waving over the centerfield scoreboard were whipping straight out. Under these conditions, routine fly balls in Wrigley Field were automatic home runs. A day like this was a pitcher's worst nightmare. Warming up in the bullpen, I could hear the sound of the flag snapping in the stiff breeze. I knew I had my work cut out for me.

Execute. No letting up. Keep the ball down. Throw strikes.

Fortunately, this is exactly what I did. And it was one of those outings where everyone else on my team did their jobs flawlessly. Defensively, they were perfect. Offensively, we scored a few runs early in the game—always one of my favorite things. And on the mound I was locked in. Get the signal, rock, fire, reload. Get the signal, rock, fire, reload. It was a lot of work, but it was awesome.

After the game, I sat in the clubhouse, icing my arm. The other players were patting me on the back as they walked from their lockers to the showers and back. "Great job, Orel." "You really smoked 'em, Bulldog." Tommy even came over and invited me to join him and some of his friends for dinner. (You can imagine the fun of going to an Italian restaurant with Tommy Lasorda!)

"Are you comin', Bulldog?" Tommy grinned.

"Yeah, Skip, I'll be there. Thanks."

The media was all around, asking questions and congratulating me on my performance. I should have been in heaven. This was, after all, why I played—a win, satisfied teammates, and a happy manager. I'd just delivered a beauty.

But as I sat there, I was filled with an overwhelming sense of dread. I'll never forget how this felt. I should have been enjoying myself. Instead, I was scared to death. I was evaluating the situation because in four or five days I was going to have to go back to the mound and do it again.

But much more than thinking about the hard work, I was afraid that I didn't know exactly what it would take to repeat my performance. I knew I had thrown a great, two-hit shutout, but I wasn't sure how. And if I didn't know how, I was pretty sure I wouldn't be able consistently to do it again, except on raw talent or sheer luck. In that moment, I knew I could not rest on my athleticism, skills, or experience.

I should have been enjoying myself. Instead, I was scared to death.

I didn't have control over the errorless play of my teammates. I didn't have control over hitters' failure to take advantage of my pitching mistakes. But I did have control over *my* effort between games. So I decided to take control of my preparation—become a student of the game *and* myself. Every single detail of it.

This is very difficult to describe to you because it was such a powerful moment of inspiration and deep commitment. As an athlete, I knew all about the demands and pain of physical training. I had always been willing to do this. But now I was going to put that same effort into *mental* preparation. I resolved to take my performance as an athlete to the next level. I was going to physically prepare for every game and I was also going to learn how to consistently add the preparation of my mind to the preparation of my body. The destination was sound execution but the route to success was going to come from the inside.

OLD-TIMERS' GREAT SECRET

When you're a professional athlete, your career clock ticks much faster than those of the rest of the world. In what other occupations would you be considered a veteran after just five years of experience?

During my first few years in the big leagues, I remember hearing baseball old-timers say, "If I knew then what I know now, I would have done things differently. If I had this knowledge before my ability left me, I would have played a lot better." Then they'd go on to explain what life had taught them through the rigors of trial and error, of success and failure.

What I suspected was that, over their many years in the game, experience had taught them about the value of mental readiness over results—of process over success.

But that was *not* for me. I was *not* willing to wait. I knew that picking up this wisdom by osmosis or casual observation wouldn't work. This had to be a conscious, intentional decision.

Becoming a veteran in five years wasn't fast enough! I would speed up the process so that the information I received would come in plenty of time for me to use during my short window of opportunity.

I quietly made a resolution. I told only Jamie about it. I was going to be the youngest, smartest major-league pitcher ever. And I wasn't going to *hope* that it happened to me. I was going to *make* it happen. I clearly remember making this resolution.

As a low draft pick, I was determined to beat the odds against my being successful. I was determined to admit my weaknesses and work on them. Who gets better at anything if they only work on their strengths? I would be willing to risk the embarrassment of failing in front of my coaches and teammates—during practice.

Often this looked awkward as I tried new things, but that didn't matter. If someone jabbed at me because something looked bad, I'd laugh and jab back. Then I'd continue to work on fixing the problem.

> The destination was sound execution but the route to success was going to come from the inside.

After the two-hit shutout in Chicago in 1984, I decided that I would commit myself to a new level of research and preparation. Although I would always do my best in game situations, my focus would not be on the results. Giving sole attention to wins and losses meant that forces that were out of my control would victimize me. A hitter on the opposing team who was (luckily) able to connect with my best stuff or a dropped fly ball from one of my own teammates would spoil my plan. There was nothing that I could do about these things.

But centering my mind on the details of preparation, day after day, week after week, was something I could control. I would be a good student, studying and listening to everyone. In

1984, when Burt Hooton told me, "Now the work begins," this is what he was talking about.

SELF-DISCIPLINE

The idea of "Sell out to the process" has two important facets. The first is self-discipline.

As a professional athlete for over twenty years, I have always been aware of my own drive to succeed—that will to improve and to win. I've also had the chance to observe hundreds of other professional athletes. I saw some who didn't need a coach to bug them to do their work. And I saw others who only did the minimum—guys who had a hard time keeping up their regimen unless someone was looking over their shoulder.

In 1984, when Burt Hooton told me, "Now the work begins," this was what he was talking about.

If you and I could sit in the empty stands of a sports field and watch a practice—any sport at any level—we would see some of the athletes out there taking it easy. If the coach wasn't looking, they wouldn't be hustling.

And we'd see other athletes focused on what they were doing. Anyone could tell they were serious. There'd be a determination and businesslike attitude—almost a sense of pride. And they'd be working.

These athletes aren't working because someone else is watching, they're working because *they* are watching! They are monitoring themselves. Self-discipline comes from the inside.

I have talked about the importance of choosing good coaches. One of the most important things my early mentors—my parents, my grandparents, my baseball coaches—did was notice when my work was persistent. Having them say "That's the way to work" became as important to me as hearing "Good job."

Over the years I've discovered that all coaching is good coaching. I know that sounds crazy because not all the advice coaches gave me was right. When their advice was helpful, it moved me closer to success. But when their input was wrong, it eliminated an option . . . and accomplished the same purpose. I also learned to store advice—like putting my money from the Exxon station in the bank—for future withdrawals. At the pinnacle of my career, slow curveballs and change-ups were not necessary. When I got into trouble on the mound, I had the strength to overpower my opponent. But as my physical strength diminished, I went to the bank and withdrew some of those ideas from earlier coaches.

Without really understanding it, self-discipline took hold at an early age. I was not a precocious boy or a people-pleaser. In many ways, I was too immature for that. My work wasn't primarily for anyone's approval. While I was cleaning the garage or mowing the yard or vacuuming the steps, it sunk into my mind that even though work was not fun—at times it was even a pain—it was a good thing. And when the job was done well, even if no one noticed but me, it was reward enough.

If I had developed at the same pace as my friends, hard work may not have become a habit. But because I was always trying to catch up to the competition, I knew I was going to have to work hard to excel.

AND I LOVED BASEBALL

Growing up, when I was finished with my chores, I would go into the backyard and practice—often by myself. I'd throw the baseball up and hit it into the fence behind our house. I was Al Kaline. I was Hank Aaron. I was Mickey Mantle. I did this over and over and over again. Thousands of times.

No one was going to make me work harder than I was going

to make myself work. And hard work gave me great satisfaction, especially working at something I loved. These things were rooted deep in me.

In the sixteen years that followed the two-hit shutout in Chicago, I built a mind-set where every day counted. I did my best to not only pay attention to what I was doing, but searched for what else could be done. And I created a sense of urgency to learn everything I could before my physical capabilities peaked, so I could still be successful as my strength faded.

> And when the job was done well, even if no one noticed but me, it was reward enough.

If you go to a seven-thirty big-league game, you might think that the players show up at five-thirty or six-thirty. They throw their uniforms on, do a little stretching, take some BP, then go out to play the game. Well, it wasn't that way for any serious ballplayer—and everyone who made it to the big leagues was serious. Especially late bloomers!

My career as a starter centered around a five-day rotation. That meant that I had four days to work the plan. This was my routine. No one forced me to do this; it was the part that I knew I could control.

Most of the time the team bus came to the ballpark from our hotel about three and a half hours before a game. I would often take a cab and get to the park five and a half hours before game time, especially the day after a start. My most strenuous workout was this day because it was the farthest away from the next time I went to the mound. Like a marathon runner gearing up for his race, the most vigorous running comes several weeks before the race, not the day before.

On the first day after a start, my workout would last up to three and a half hours: lifting weights, shoulder exercises, abdominals, stretching, an hour of cardiovascular work, and light throwing.

The next day wasn't as tough. There was more stretching, massage, sprint work, and twenty minutes of throwing on the side. The next day was back to heavy work, more like day one. The final day before the start was very light, maybe just breaking a sweat.

Then, before my start there was stretching and massage and I was ready to warm up in the bullpen.

I went through this regimen hundreds of times. Unless I specifically asked for it, no one followed me around to make sure I did the work. Because process was more important than results, self-discipline refused to cut corners or give up. I wasn't willing to let those results—good or bad—change my intensity, concentration, or preparation for the next event.

SELF-EXAMINATION

The second facet in the process is self-examination.

As a professional athlete, one of the benefits my career provided me was that I always had someone evaluating my performance. From the time I was in Little League, I had coaches working with me. For over thirty years, I relied on the knowledge and expertise of someone alongside me. Their unbiased opinion was based on what they were seeing, and the moment they saw something that needed adjustment they'd tell me what they saw.

Because process was more important than results, self-discipline refused to cut corners or give up.

As a major leaguer, I had pitching coaches whose only job was to study my mechanics—the windup, the transfer of my weight, the position of my shoulders, the angle of my arm at release, the follow through . . .

everything imaginable. Their brutal honesty with me was what I hoped for.

When you watch a baseball game on television, you often see shots of the manager and coaches standing around the dugout. Except for adjusting their caps, chewing on sunflower seeds or, like Dusty Baker in San Francisco, working nonstop on a toothpick, it may look like these men are leisurely watching the game just like everyone else.

This is far from the truth.

These men are watching their players' every move. Managers are thinking through each and every possible game situation that could arise. Batting coaches are analyzing swings and preparing the hitters for their next AB. Pitching coaches are studying every movement of their hurlers. Visits to the mound were often exactly what I needed to make a slight adjustment to an immediate problem. My coaches were watching and they knew how to help.

The only exceptions to this were when a pitching coach came to the mound because his pitcher was in trouble and the manager wanted to give the reliever a few extra minutes to warm up . . . or if Tommy Lasorda was involved. Sometimes, when I was with the Dodgers, Tommy would explode about something and send my pitching coach, Ron Perranoski, to the mound.

"Go talk to him," Tommy would howl. Perry knew better than to ask why, so he'd ask for time and hustle out of the dugout to talk to me.

"I'm out here 'cause Tommy told me to come talk to you," Perry would say with a smirk. "He's a little fired up. I don't know what to tell ya, so I'll just stand here for a while." Before turning to go, sometimes he'd add, "Since I'm here, slow your leg kick down a little. That should help you keep the ball down."

He'd give me an encouraging pat and walk back to the dugout.

Coaches helped me to get a better look at what I was doing.

And the secret was to submit to the honesty and work ethic of my toughest coach: myself.

spitter? Hershiser doesn't throw a spitter," he quipped. "How do I know? I've seen the movement of his pitches during warm-ups. Who cheats when you're warming up? Who loads it up in the bullpen?"

Whitey was right. Even though I was tempted, I never intentionally marked the ball. Why? Was it because I was afraid of getting caught? No. I didn't throw a spitter because I wanted my "talk" to be consistent with my "walk." Winning by cheating didn't carry any value. Success wasn't worth anything if I broke the rules. So I didn't do it.

And what about the umpires? What does self-examination look like when it comes to submitting to authority? Ever since my years in Little League, I'd learned something about umpires: their authority was ultimate and absolute. They were the boss and, as a player, my responsibility was to submit to that authority, which I decided to do.

And even though there were many calls I completely disagreed with and many times I wanted to dispute the call, I knew that an argument would contradict my decision to submit to that authority. Sometimes, after a "bad" call I'd walk around behind the mound for a while to blow off some steam, but I didn't argue. Well, maybe a little—but never so much that I got ejected from the game.

Talking about truthful self-examination also reminds me of the many tests I faced outside the lines. Like fidelity. Spending thousands of nights by myself on the road provided ample opportunities. Was I tempted? Yes. Could I have gotten away with it? Maybe. Did I give in? No. Why?

As I took an honest look at myself, I wanted to see a man who was not only faithful to his trusting wife, but also a man who was obedient to his own vows and promises. On February 7,

There were also video replays . . . sometimes in slow moti
Over and over again my work was examined, building me t
ward the goal of being the best I could be. I watched thes
videos, reaping the most I could from what they revealed.
watched them with my coaches and I watched them alone.

After years of this detailed examination, something interesting began to happen. I realized that in my mind's eye I could see myself without coaches and without videotape. I had felt and visualized my mechanics in such detail that I could actually "watch" what I was doing as if I were someone else watching me do it. When a coach suggested a change, I could make the adjustment, execute the pitch, then "watch" to see if I had done the right thing.

NOT WORTH LYING TO MYSELF

In baseball, I learned the importance of being brutally honest. What good would it do if I tried to fool myself? Like cheating at solitaire. Once I had done my work and given myself a grade, then I set out to refine the new goal. And the secret was to submit to the honesty and work ethic of my toughest coach: myself.

Talking about truthful self-examination reminds me of the many tests I faced along the way between the lines. Like throwing a spitter.

It's against the rules of baseball for a pitcher to intentionally tamper with the ball. A cut from a sharp belt buckle or a scratch from sandpaper on the surface of the ball will change its flight, making it more difficult for the batter to hit. Early in my career I was accused of breaking this rule—of cheating. The action on my sinker convinced the opposition that I was doing something to the ball. This was, of course, a compliment.

While he was the manager of the St. Louis Cardinals, Whitey Herzog was asked if he thought I tampered with the ball. "A

1981, I told Jamie that I would always love her and that I would be honorable. I made this solemn oath in a church—a holy place. I gave her my word in the presence of God and my family and friends. Marital fidelity was what I had promised. In addition to the fact that I love Jamie and knew she loved me, that promise was enough, even when we disagreed.

"Commitment . . . yuk," we used to tease after heated arguments.

Selling out to the process included a lifetime of self-examination. I had promised myself that I wouldn't be satisfied with any discrepancy, so I did my best to continue to pursue high standards.

Several years ago a reporter was asking me about my baseball career. Halfway into the interview, he asked me a question that was out of the rhythm of the conversation: "You're a religious man, aren't you?"

> Success wasn't worth anything if I broke the rules. So I didn't do it.

Although I don't remember my exact answer to this question, the gist of it was something like this.

> If you're asking me if there is just a part of me that includes God, I'd have to say no. If you're asking if there are certain religious ceremonies that I include in my day in order to be obedient to God, I'd say no again. But if you're asking if I have a personal relationship with God that I try to allow to affect everything I think, say, and do, then I'd say yes.

After a short pause, the reporter went back to his scripted questions.

TAKING INVENTORY

When I worked for my dad at his printing company, I learned the importance of keeping an accurate assessment of inventory. Running out of supplies in the middle of a printing job would have definitely slowed things down and my head would have probably rolled.

For me, one of the most important elements of "Sell out to the process" has been a constant program of taking inventory.

When I was in a slump, I reviewed what I was doing. I did my best to stay on my regimen. I asked the medical staff questions about my workouts to be sure I wasn't missing something. I asked my coaches if there was anything in my mechanics that they thought could be adjusted. I thought about my sleeping and eating habits. I looked at videotape. I tried to leave no stone unturned.

> Selling out to the process included a lifetime of self-examination.

And during hot streaks—like winning five games during the month of May in 1998—I was just as diligent about taking inventory. I examined the process with as much dedication as I did when the results were bad.

"If it ain't broke," some people say, "don't fix it."

This was not the way I thought. Because the process was more important than the results, I did my best to not allow success to overshadow my regular examination of what I was doing . . . and how I was doing it. I didn't want complacency to creep in. The focus was on the process and the goal was to make hot streaks last as long as possible and to shorten cold streaks.

There's an old wive's tale in sports that when things are going well, you do not evaluate, review, or think about it. If you do, you might blow it.

But I believed that the risk of shortening a hot streak by continuing to analyze it was well worth it. I knew that the information I collected during this evaluation of the good times could be used to shorten a cold streak later. This gave me the blueprint I needed to go back and recreate the success.

During the '88 season, as I was getting close to the one pitching record that everyone—including me—thought was unbreakable, I remember teammates and reporters tiptoeing around the subject. Somehow they thought they might jinx me if they'd say something about my scoreless inning streak. I didn't worry about this.

I reviewed everything I was doing with my trainers and coaches. My commitment to the daily process had gotten me to this point. And if I had a shot at breaking Drysdale's record, it's what would take me the rest of the way. Fortunately, it worked out.

BUT THAT WAS BASEBALL. WHAT ABOUT LIFE?

For me, these self-examination and self-discipline principles are exactly the same off the field.

The ability to honestly see yourself act, hear yourself talk, see the look on your own face, and answer the question "What's it like to live with me?" is a very useful thing. And the way to make sure you're seeing it accurately is to check with your family and friends. Ask them what I used to ask my pitching coaches. "What do you see in me? Does this look right? What do you think?"

Then humbly listen to what they say. Work on what they advise. Even get to the place where you can anticipate, seeing yourself without their input.

> See yourself act, hear yourself talk, see the look on your own face, and answer the question "What's it like to live with me?"

I assure you that this was easier for me on the field than it is off the field. But in the same way that I loved hearing "Now that's the way to work" from my dad or my coaches, I am thankful that my family and friends know that even when I fail, my goal is to never stop selling out to self-discipline and self-examination.

PRINCIPLE #4

Excellence Matters

I am a tremendously competitive person. By my appearance, this comes as a surprise to some. And why not? I have a funny name. In a baseball uniform I look like I have no chest—like I could palm a basketball with my shoulders. Even though I'm 6'3" and weigh something in the neighborhood of 210 pounds, my lanky arms and legs don't reveal much strength. Because of my reddish hair and toothy grin, I've been described as Howdy Doody, a professor, or a young Ronnie Howard.

Soon after being chosen as the 1988 Sportsman of the Year, I told *Sports Illustrated,* "Let's face it. I'm just a pale guy with glasses, long arms, and a sunken chest. I look like I work in a flour factory and have never lifted a weight."

A fierce competitor? I don't think so.

But these looks were misleading. Deep inside was a tenacious will to succeed—to do better than anyone would ever expect . . . to pursue excellence. The heart transplant that Tommy wished on me (taking his out and giving it to me) was not necessary at all. "Bulldog" or not, intensity in my performance on the field and the will to do my best were as much a part of my heritage

> Deep inside was a tenacious will to succeed—to do better than anyone would ever expect.

and genetic makeup as any of these more visible, less intimidating, physical characteristics.

Watching my dad take over the kitchen while making his gravy for Yorkshire pudding at our traditional family Christmas dinner is a snapshot of what I'm talking about. He is festive and all, but it's like Julia Child meets George Patton, if you know what I mean. "We're going to make this gravy. It will be as good as any we've ever had, even better than last year. And it will be hot, flawless, and right on time. Any questions?"

This drive to succeed—an unwillingness to be content with the status quo—coupled with the support of coaches who shouted their encouragement or instructions from the sidelines, gave me the desire to not only do my best, but to actually surprise people who were watching from the stands. To try to do everything well.

Thorough preparation was non-negotiable, but excellence was always the goal. I know this may sound like a contradiction to what I've said about the importance of selling out to the process, but it's not.

THE GAME FACE

There's no way of guessing how many questions beat reporters and sportscasters asked me over the years, but I'm sure they number in the thousands. Sometimes these questions were fairly mindless, like "So, where did you grow up?" and "Where did you play college ball?" (they could have gotten this information from the media guide). Another annoying question went something like "Did you hang that slider to McGwire?"

In fact, during the 1998 season I did hang a slider to Mark

McGwire during a regular season inter-league game in Cleveland. Sometimes when a hitter makes solid contact, you see a pitcher turn around to watch the fly ball, hoping it stays in the park. Not this time. The instant the ball left Mark's bat, I knew it was gone. Like a spectator, I turned and gasped as it headed for the stands. In fact, the whole stadium gasped. In just a few seconds the ball collided with the huge Budweiser sign, sixty rows over the left-field bleachers. It made a huge bang, leaving a baseball-sized dent.

As McGwire rounded third, Cleveland fans gave him an ovation. Cleveland fans. Actually, I thought about applauding, too. But I didn't.

The next day Bart Swain, the Indians' assistant PR director, came to the clubhouse to tell me that the official scorekeeper in the booth had estimated the drive at 457 feet. "But," he said, "there are a bunch of us who think it went over five hundred." With a smile, I thanked him for keeping this estimate to himself.

> Thorough preparation was non-negotiable, but excellence was always the goal.

The same day, as the team was out on the field before BP, Sandy Alomar, my catcher, snuck up to the last row of bleacher seats in left center field. Getting as close as he could to the now-famous dent in the Budweiser sign, he shouted, "Wow, man. This is a long way up here . . . a reeeeeally long way." Everybody turned to see him, waving his arms and yelling. "Hey guys, look up here."

We all laughed like crazy. I didn't mind. I really was still quite amazed myself. If you're going to give 'em up, you might as well enjoy 'em. For a pitcher, there's nothing worse than yielding a home run that scrapes the back of the wall.

Anyway, sometimes reporters asked good questions—tough questions—like the ones that caused me to reflect on the part of

> If you're going to give 'em up, you might as well enjoy 'em.

the game that I loved. The thinking part. Many of these questions were about my preparation, my focus, or my game face. Reporters were often curious about my sober countenance and where it came from. And they wanted to know about the intensity I showed when I walked out to the mound to start a game—I did this 465 more times after Tommy announced "You've got the ball" in 1984.

Here's what I told them.

From the first moment I opened my eyes the morning of a start, I had tunnel vision aimed at my task for that day. I could not allow any interruptions or distractions into my thinking. Game day is sacred for the starting pitcher and everyone in baseball knows it. On this day, I was completely on my own—from determining the time I'd get up to when and what I'd eat to all my pregame preparation at the ballpark. No one would interrupt my routine.

In the clubhouse, it was understood that you didn't speak to the starting pitcher unless you were spoken to. This was my day. And my face told you everything you needed to know. But what about games on the road? Fans love to get inside your head and upset your routine and your concentration.

About half of my starts were in front of hometown crowds who were hoping that I would do well. I loved the loud cheering and support. You can't imagine how awesome it was to walk onto the field and be met by forty thousand "friends"!

But the other 50 percent of my starts were on the road in front of fans who wanted me to bomb. My goal in these two settings was pretty simple: to do my best and to win. But my mind-set was that I wanted to reward the hometown crowd by doing better than they'd hoped for, sending them home very happy. And I wanted to reward the crowds on the road with a very bad day for their team. I made their discomfort my goal. I even turned derogatory remarks from unruly fans into personal encouragement and motivation. The worse their hollering got, the more fired up I got!

Behind my game face was intense focus. I had completed the process of being prepared for this moment and would not be satisfied with anything but excellence in the execution of every single pitch.

These thoughts were in constant play during the regular season. But they really intensified during the post-season.

THE 1995 WORLD SERIES—GAME FIVE

Expectations were high as I faced one of the most important games of my career in the 1995 World Series. To say that I was focused and ready would definitely describe my state of mind. I was starting against the Braves. Greg Maddux and I had faced each other in Game One and I had taken the loss. More than anything I wanted to even the score against Greg and the Braves. (Maddux had just completed a great season and was headed for his fourth National League Cy Young Award.)

My teammates and I were hanging out in the clubhouse before the game. During the time right before a big game some of the guys sit quietly, some listen to music on their headphones, others read the scouting reports, and a few play cards. There's very little chatter going on. I had gotten to the ballpark in plenty of time to go through my usual pregame routine. Down three games to one in the Series, this was a must win. Given what had happened with my outing in the

I even turned derogatory remarks from unruly fans into personal encouragement and motivation.

first game, I was meticulous in my preparation, to say the least. My game face was firmly in place.

One of the clubhouse kids walked over to my locker, interrupting my train of thought with the news that I had a phone call. *Who's calling me now? This is a bad time for a phone call,* I remember thinking as I stood up to get the phone. Jamie, my sons, and my close friends knew that bothering me this close to a start—especially one as important as this—wasn't a good idea. In fact, I almost sat back down and told the kid to take a message.

"I think it's Tommy Lasorda," he said, knowing by my expression that I was about to not take the call.

I wonder what Tommy wants. I walked across the clubhouse and picked up the phone.

"Hello."

"Bulldog, this is Tommy."

"Hey, Skip," I answered, a little confused to hear from my former manager. I started to ask how he was doing but something told me that Tommy wasn't listening. Tommy was talking. From years of experience, I knew better than to try to talk when Tommy had something to say, so I closed my mouth and opened my ear.

"I watched your last game, Bulldog. What's the matter with you? You didn't look like a bulldog; you looked like a Chihuahua. Klesko gets up there in the seventh and you walk him. McGriff comes to the plate and you walk him, too. Then you let 'em take you out of the game."

I wanted to explain what had happened, but there was no room for my words on the phone line. With Tommy talking, it was plenty crowded already.

"You didn't believe in your stuff," he continued. "You started aimin' the ball. You were thinkin' too much. Get out there tonight and let it all hang out. I want you to have that fire in your eyes."

His voice dropped just a little, letting me know that he was getting ready to deliver the clincher.

> You didn't look like a bulldog; you looked like a Chihuahua.

"Orel," Tommy said in that familiar voice, "I wanna see the Bulldog."

I don't know if I said anything. I don't even remember hanging up the phone. Tommy was the only person in the world with the courage to actually call me at this moment and I'm glad he did. I felt energized, pumped up . . . with a new focus. Tommy was looking for that guy who would take five punches just to deliver one. I was that guy.

Actually, I was pumped. I walked back to my locker, but I was too fired up to sit down. I couldn't wait to get to the mound. I was so psyched that even though the game didn't start for almost two hours, it seemed only a few minutes until we were on the field facing the Braves in Game Five of the World Series.

Even now, the highlights of this game make me smile.

I got the Braves out in order in the top of the first. We scored two runs in the bottom of the inning. The Braves scored once in the fourth and once again in the fifth. We scored two more in the bottom of the sixth.

In the eighth inning, leading 4-2, I gave up a hit to Mike Mordecai, the first hitter I faced in the inning. Mordecai had been brought in as a pinch hitter for Maddux. The Braves needed a rally and Mordecai had gotten one started. The next batter was Marquis Grissom, a strong first-pitch, fastball hitter. I challenged him with a fastball and, sure enough, he hit a screaming line drive right back to the mound. I threw my glove hand across my body, speared the ball, and fired a throw over to Paul Sorrento at first to double up Mordecai. Two outs, nobody on. The Cleveland fans went nuts.

I circled around behind the mound, yelling to myself, "Take that! Take that! Take that!" This was like throwing the knockout punch in a prizefight. In that moment, I released all my stored up energy from losing Game One, the intense preparation of the past four days, and Tommy's pregame phone call. My teammates and I were going to win this game and take the Series back to Atlanta for Game Six. (Unfortunately, we lost Game Six on Tom Glavine's masterpiece—a one-hit shutout—to lose the Series.)

> I circled around behind the mound, yelling to myself, "Take that! Take that! Take that!"

PARALYSIS BY ANALYSIS

When Tommy told me that I was "thinking too much" he was referring to the first game of the Series.

Atlanta's Greg Maddux and I were each trying to give our teams a head start toward winning a World Series ring by capturing the first game. It was the bottom of the seventh inning with the game tied at one when I walked Ryan Klesko and Fred McGriff, two of the Braves' biggest hitters. The walks were not intentional, of course. But rather than challenging them with my best stuff, as Tommy had said on the phone, I was too careful and lost them both. Now they were standing at first and second with no outs.

Mark "Wiles" Wiley, my pitching coach, asked for time-out and walked to the mound. My mind was racing.

I can go on, but it's late in the game and I know I'm down to my last few batters. The way Maddux is pitching, we can't afford to give the Braves any more runs. I'm not scared but Chipper Jones is coming up and I'm not the best guy for this situation. I've lost my release point and there's no time to try and find it. We need our best now and I'm not it. I guess that's what I need to tell Wiles.

"How do you feel?" Wiles asked as he stepped up on the mound, never expecting to hear what I was about to say.

"I think you should take me out," I said. Wiles and I stood there for a moment. We didn't say anything.

Actually, I was surprised that Mark Wiley looked so surprised. All year, he and Grover (Mike Hargrove, our manager) had trusted me to tell them exactly how I felt on the mound. I knew these men—and my teammates—had a great deal of confidence in me. But in that moment on the mound, something happened that I'll never forget. Looking back I realized that instead of trusting the process and pursuing excellence, I had crowded my mind with questions and doubts. Rather than trusting my instincts and pushing through my fears, I allowed the negative to overwhelm the possible positive solution.

Watching the game on television three thousand miles from Atlanta, this subtle shift in my thinking did not escape Tommy. He knew me well enough to know how to push my buttons. During the ten years I had played for him, he would have called time-out, marched to the mound, and gotten in my face.

"I don't care what you think about getting this hitter out," he would have announced, his nose only a few inches from mine. "Follow your fingers, Bulldog, and just let it go. I don't care about anything else. I want to see everything you have." Then he would have stopped talking and looked straight into my eyes for just a moment to be sure I heard every word he said.

"I'll do the managing. You pitch."

With that he would have turned and walked back to the dugout.

But now, instead of being pushed by a manager in my face or an internal desire to succeed, I was overtaken by a craving to protect my team. When I reached the dugout, I could tell by the way my team-

Rather than trusting my instincts and pushing through my fears, I allowed the negative to overwhelm the possible positive solution.

mates acted that they were disappointed in me. Their looks let me know they thought I had given up. They didn't understand that I had made the decision with their best interests at heart, although that still didn't make it right.

Grover brought Paul Assenmacher in from the bullpen. A sacrifice bunt, an intentional walk, a sacrifice fly, and a suicide squeeze and we were down 3-1. As it turned out, even though we eked out a run in the top of the ninth, that moment on the mound with Mark Wiley had been the turning point in the game. Atlanta won 3-2.

Early the next morning I read the account in the paper. Over the years of playing in the majors, this was always an interesting experience, especially after a loss in the World Series. Reporters had talked to Grover and Wiles about what had happened.

"Sometimes Hershiser thinks too much," Mike Hargrove had told the media.

I remember being upset. *What's this about?* I remember thinking to myself. *You're back-stabbing me, you know. Should I say something to Grover?*

Fortunately, I didn't talk to anyone. I took a cab from the hotel to Fulton County Stadium early for my usual post-start workout. Over the next few hours my mind retraced the events of the night before. And I was glad that I hadn't mentioned anything about it.

Grover had been right. I had blown it and I needed to learn from the experience. Tommy's phone call cemented the change I needed to make. His timely challenge got my attention and released the competitor inside me. His pointed pregame airing out changed my thinking.

Trying to avoid failure never works as well as taking what you've learned, trusting your instincts, and boldly stepping out to give it all you can. Preparation creates confidence. Process leads to sound execution. Regimen aims effort toward perfection. Excellence matters.

This was a great lesson.

THE MANY FACES OF EXCELLENCE

Sometimes excellence looks like winning and celebration. And sometimes it doesn't.

After the 1999 season with the Mets, there was a lot of uncertainty in my life. Not only had the Mets informed me that they weren't going to exercise their option for 2000, but because of the awful plane crash, Robert Fraley, my representative and trusted advisor, was gone. What was I going to do? Who would want a forty-one-year-old pitcher?

In late November I got calls from Kevin Malone, the general manager of the Dodgers, and Davey Johnson, the team's manager. They told me that the Dodgers were very interested in my "coming home." Over the next few weeks, I received other offers, but the thought of going back to Los Angeles where I had started my major league career sounded pretty exciting.

> Preparation creates confidence. Process leads to sound execution. Regimen aims effort toward perfection.

I even got a call from Tommy Lasorda, who was a VP in the Dodgers' front office. As you might imagine, Tommy was eager to have me back in Dodger blue.

Kevin and Davey's offer to play in Los Angeles again was hard to turn down. Bob Daly, the new owner, was very supportive. And Tommy's enthusiastic encouragement was impossible to deny. I signed with the Dodgers in December.

Spring Training back in Vero Beach two months later went very well. It had been six years since I had last been in Dodgertown and it was great to be back.

Knowing what my aging body was up against, I worked harder than I had worked in sixteen years. I felt strong on the mound. At the close of Spring Training, my ERA was under 2, the best on the staff.

The Dodgers were expecting a forty-one-year-old veteran. They got more than they bargained for. I was feeling good and ready for a great season.

I flew to Los Angeles and for the first few weeks of the season lived with our good friends, Randy and Robin Northrup. When the boys finished school, Jamie and I found a house to rent in Pasadena. We confidently signed a lease through the end of October. We were hoping for a long and successful season.

Our older son, Quinton (who was fifteen at the time), got an internship in the Dodgers' Public Relations office. Jordan, at eleven, was able to do some work in the clubhouse and was the batboy for several home games. Jamie was back in Southern California where we had lived for ten years and was renewing old friendships and enjoying her old stomping ground. Everything was great.

The Dodgers were expecting a forty-one-year-old veteran. They got more than they bargained for.

On April 14, I started in the home opener against Cincinnati. The first game of the new millennium; a newly refurbished stadium; and a full house of screaming Dodger faithful were indescribable. Although it felt like I was struggling, I finished six strong innings before Terry Adams came in from the bullpen in relief. When Barry Larkin grounded out in the top of the ninth, we had won the game and I had notched number 204 in my career.

I never could have guessed that this would be my last career win.

As the season began to unfold, the uncertainty I had felt in that first home game began to increase. Although I did experience some of the usual aches and pains, the lack of success wasn't due to any injury. All I can say is that, even though I didn't let up on my regimen, I didn't have what it took to get hitters out.

Davey took me out of the starting rotation. Going to the bull-pen and contributing to the team as a reliever was something I was willing to do. What I hadn't counted on was how the change in schedule would affect everything.

For sixteen years, I had essentially executed the same routine. I had built a strategy that took me through the five days from start to start. I knew exactly what to do on each of these days: cardiovascular workout every day, weights every other day, stretching every day, massage every other day, and vitamins and health shakes timed perfectly. Young guys can shortcut routines and abuse their bodies, but as I got older, all of these things became even more important to my success as I got ready to go out and pitch on that fifth day.

As a reliever, all of this routine changed. I didn't know when I'd get the call. Sometimes I'd pitch on consecutive days, then wait for ten days to pitch again. This destroyed my workout pattern. It was a much bigger adjustment than I'd expected. It also invaded my consistent mental approach. Going to the ballpark every day but not knowing exactly what I was going to do took its toll on my body and on me. All of this came on very quickly.

But I was holding a place on the Dodgers' twenty-five-man roster. They expected twenty-five active, productive players and I wasn't willing to go along for the ride as a noncontributing member of the team. I wasn't any help at the big-league level and I knew it.

Davey did everything he could to keep me in a routine. "We'll have a few innings of a simulated game every five days," he told me. "You can throw full speed to your teammates." But it didn't work.

At the end of May, Davey and I had a conversation. "Send me down," I began. "I'll go to San Bernadino (the Dodgers' single A team). I'll go do my starter thing and get back into my regimen in A-ball. Then, after three or four starts, I'll be back. It'll be like a mini Spring Training in the middle of the season. Then I'll be ready to help you."

Davey agreed to the plan.

For eighteen days I drove to San Bernadino. It felt great to get back into my old routine. And I did well, winning all four starts. This was very encouraging to me so I told Davey that I was ready to go. That was the good news.

But this was A-ball, three levels down from the majors. These hitters were very different from the hitters in the big leagues. That was the bad news.

> I wasn't any help at the big-league level and I knew it.

On June 26 I walked to the mound for a start against San Diego. I knew that my manager, my coaches, and my teammates were pulling for me. The fans were enthusiastic. Jamie was there, adding her support. I truly believed that I could pitch at this level again. But it wasn't to be.

With two outs in the second inning and eight earned runs on the board, Davey walked to the mound. He had done everything in his power to let me finish the inning so he wouldn't have to come out and take me out of the game in front of the fans. But I was in too much trouble for him to wait.

"This is it," I said handing him the baseball for the last time. "You're going to have to release me. I think it's over." He nodded, knowing that I didn't just mean this game against the Padres. As I walked to the dugout, the fans stood to cheer, even though my performance had almost sealed a loss for their team. They knew, too.

I walked into Davey's office after the game and agreed to a release from the Dodgers. Tommy came to the clubhouse. He knew that it was time for me to hang it up. He hugged me and we cried like little boys. It was over.

A week later, on July 6, a telephone press conference was arranged and I officially retired. Were there other opportunities with other major league teams to keep my career going? Yes.

But I knew it was time. And as painful as it was after almost seventeen years, I walked away from the game I loved.

Even in calling it quits, my goal was excellence. I had taken time to carefully review the past two months. I had consulted with my family and close friends. I had prayed, asking God for wisdom and assurance. Now it was time to go.

WHAT I'LL MISS MOST

Many questions were asked over the phone at my retirement press conference about what I was going to do. At the time, I was in a mild state of shock. I had several different options to sort through, so I told the reporters the truth. "I don't know what I'll be doing—inside or outside of baseball."

Toward the end of the call, one reporter spoke up. "Orel, now that you're retiring, what are you going to miss the most?"

I wasn't prepared for this question, but as I look back, it was the best one of the day.

It was a surreal moment, almost as though everything dropped into slow motion. I closed my eyes, envisioning the faces of the men and women—most of them familiar—who were on the phone, covering the story. I knew this was the last time I would be talking to them as a player. I thought of the privilege I had enjoyed of living my dream—of playing in the majors and having succeeded. I knew how much I'd miss the games, working on strategies, the camaraderie in the clubhouse, the cheers from loyal fans, even the rigors of my daily workouts. I opened my mouth to speak, almost as though I were in some sort of zone, somewhere else.

> Tommy came to the clubhouse. He hugged me and we cried like little boys. It was over.

"I'll miss holding the ball," I said.

The feel of the baseball in my hand had been the focus of my career. From the time I'd played catch with my dad, I had known its wonderful familiarity. For over thirty years the baseball had shaped my activities and focused my competitive spirit. I had walked onto the field as a skinny kid from New Jersey, had the privilege of making a contribution to the game, and now was walking away for the last time.

I felt like an artist stricken with blindness or a speaker losing his voice. My eyes welled up with tears at the finality of the moment. In the silence, the reporters—even the most seasoned among them—seemed to understand and allowed me my moment.

> "I'll miss holding the ball," I said.

In the months that followed my retirement, I was forced to face life from a different perspective. Some days were exciting as I plotted out a new course. And some days were very difficult.

But I was determined to do my best to take the same approach that I had taken when I started playing baseball. I was going to continue to look for good coaches to believe in. Knowing that life will always be filled with the unpredictable, I wanted to keep selling out to the process. And, faced with the temptations of mediocrity, I would continue to believe that excellence still mattered.

THE GIFT OF "IT"

Two months after I retired from baseball, my son Jordan received a notice in the mail to sign up for fall Little League baseball. When I saw the flyer on the kitchen table, it hit me. Why not sign up to manage Jordan's Little League team?

Less than a year after I battled on the field to help the Mets to the play-offs, I was standing on a Little League field coaching eleven- and twelve-year-olds, including my own Jordan. And wouldn't you know it, our team was the Dodgers! As I stood on the mound, helping young hurlers with their mechanics or infielders with their routine (glove down, charge the ball), memories of my own early years in the game came flooding back.

> Why not sign up to manage Jordan's Little League team?

I was grateful for the coaches who had willingly given of their time to teach me the basics: Dave Betz, Mike Griffith, Bob Atkins, and of course my dad. They inspired me to work hard, taking batting practice until my hands were raw. Watching the boys on my Little League team, I recalled times when, as a kid, I had felt so bad because I had made the game-losing error or struck out in a crucial moment. I could still see my folks in the stands, cheering for me. I remembered Popsicles and post-game trips to the A&W root beer stand. Those are some great memories.

Mostly, I was thankful for the gift of "it," because I had the privilege of running a Little League team where some of the boys had "it." They came to games early so they could take extra BP. They hustled to their places on the field. They dove for fly balls and grounders. They encouraged their teammates. As a youngster, I had been given the gift of "it."

You've heard people speak of "it"—in sports and in life.

"That boy playing shortstop, he's got it."

"That young girl playing the piano, she's got what it takes."

"That person has it all together."

Call it the drive to succeed, the will to win, or the desire for excellence, I had been given it. Parents, grandparents, teachers, coaches, managers, even teammates and friends—these people had poured into me that competitive edge. Over and over I heard them say, "That may be good enough for some kids, but it's not good enough for you. Orel, you can do better."

A psychologist was recently quoted as saying that children do not build self-esteem from play. They build it from work. Even though baseball was a game to be "played," without really knowing it, I had turned it into "work."

Back then, it may have been a stretch—a statement of hope—when people told me I had it. Amazingly enough, I was naïve enough to believe them.

Even though baseball was a game to be "played," without really knowing it, I had turned it into "work."

They gave it to me. I kept it. And it has served me very well.

From the time I was a little boy, I knew that I couldn't be like some of the other kids and wait for life to come to me. I would not be satisfied with that. Excellence mattered. It was my goal. So I went for it.

PRINCIPLE #5

Balance Is Key

It's almost impossible to describe what happened to my family and me during the final months of the '88 season. In spite of seeing my face on the cover of magazines and hearing my name every day on radio and television, I still saw myself as exactly the same. But my family and I were treated very differently. This had the potential to throw me completely off balance.

Before breaking the scoreless inning streak and living through the unbelievable post-season, we were able to live fairly normal lives. Sure, I'd be recognized in LA or occasionally someone would spot me sitting in a restaurant in a National League city. But after the huge publicity in '88, everything changed.

Our first experience of this was moments after our team plane arrived at LAX about 2:00 A.M. on October 21, 1988, following the final World Series game in Oakland. It was the middle of the night so we only expected a few reporters and a handful of die-hard fans to be at the airport. Just before getting off the plane we were told that the fans who *had* arrived were not being allowed into the airport.

As we stepped from the jetway into the airport, Jamie and I—and the rest of my teammates—were surrounded by the media. Reporters shoved microphones in our direction and bright lights flooded the area. As they asked us questions, we slowly moved down the concourse toward the place where we were scheduled to meet our limo.

> In spite of seeing my face on the cover of magazines and hearing my name every day on radio and television, I still saw myself as exactly the same.

When my teammates and I got to the front of the airport, policemen and security guards guided us toward the doors leading outside. A large space had been roped off from the crowd so the team could safely get to the bus. Our private car had also been allowed to wait in this secure place. Knowing this, when a policeman spotted Jamie and me, he offered to escort us through a different set of doors and directly to our waiting car. Unfortunately, he miscalculated. Instead of opening doors that led us to our limo, we stepped into the middle of thousands of screaming Dodger fans. This was a big mistake.

There was a frenzy of pushing and shoving like I had never seen. When they realized that I was there, right in the middle of the crowd, they pressed toward us. Well-meaning and very excited fans stuck out their hands and hollered my name. Some reached in to touch us and others pulled on our clothing. People tousled my hair, shouting things like, "Yea, Orel!" and "Way to go, Bulldog!"

I could tell that some of these guys had come directly from celebrations at their favorite hangouts.

With all the commotion I couldn't imagine that we'd be able to make it to our car. The officer just kept trying to guide us through the crowd. In the crush, Jamie lost her shoe, but we continued on; I would have been trampled on the street trying to find it. Although no one meant us any harm, this was getting pretty hairy.

Knowing that we'd have to go to Plan B, the police officer shoved us into a nearby courtesy van and barked an order to the driver. "Take the Hershisers wherever they need to go." With wide eyes, the driver complied and slowly started to move through the crowd. My heart was pounding. Jamie was in tears. What was meant to be a welcome-home celebration had turned into a harrowing experience for both of us.

People surrounded the van, pounding out their enthusiasm on the windows, rocking it back and forth. The driver frantically called his dispatcher. With all the noise, we couldn't hear exactly what he said, but the response came back over the loudspeakers.

"Take them home . . . and get two autographs for my sons."

The driver continued to ease his van through the crowd. The pounding and shaking persisted. At that moment, we heard someone banging on the window right next to us. By the sound, we knew he was using something that could break the window. When I looked up, I saw a man hitting the window with Jamie's shoe. It was completely mangled, the heel broken and hanging by a thread.

In the crush, Jamie lost her shoe, but we continued on; I would have been trampled on the street trying to find it.

I slid the window down just a few inches so I could hear his voice. "Is this your wife's shoe?" he hollered above the noise.

"Yeah, thanks." I took what was left of the shoe and slid the window back up.

Jamie and I looked at the shoe and started to laugh. "Wow," I joked. "Sorry about your shoe."

Once the courtesy van had made its way through the mob, Jamie and I sat for a while, holding each other. Then, all alone in our makeshift limo that probably had never been driven at freeway speeds, we talked about what had just happened. Sure, we were excited. But we also knew that maintaining stability in all of this commotion—for ourselves and for the boys—was going to be a huge challenge. We really didn't know it then, but our lives would never be the same.

I had reached the absolute pinnacle of the baseball world. Now I was faced with a new life goal: continuing to keep balance in our lives.

As a professional, I already knew that balance was critical to a successful athletic career. I had to find equilibrium in my sleeping habits, my food intake, my workout regimen, my mechanics on the mound, and not being solely focused on wins and losses.

Now, in the same way, our family needed to find a way of maintaining solid ground and *staying* balanced.

This huge challenge was going to be helped by the fact that nine years earlier I had found a faith that provided me *inner* peace and stability.

INTERNAL BALANCE

Once I had committed to the Dodgers in 1979, my first assignment was their Class A club in Clinton, Iowa. During that season I went 4-0 and was selected, along with my teammate Butch Wickensheimer, to go to the Arizona Instructional League in the fall. This was a big deal for both of us, since only a few players from each minor league team were invited. The Buckaroo Hotel in Scottsdale would be my home for the next few months. I asked Butch to be my roommate.

Butch was a nice guy and I knew we'd get along. I was also intrigued with him because I knew that he was a Christian. During that summer in Clinton, I sometimes saw him reading his Bible by the overhead light riding on the team bus after a night game. Sometimes he'd have to move to a different seat because most of the lights on those busses didn't work (remember this is Class A baseball!).

We kidded him about being religious and he took it in stride. He wasn't obnoxious about his faith, and there was something about Butch's life that was compelling to me.

I knew about God and the Bible, but I had never given it much thought. I asked Butch what he saw in his Bible. "Everything," he told me. This fascinated me. For weeks I barraged him with questions. He kept referring to answers that came from his Bible. So, late one night at the Buckaroo, I pulled the Gideon Bible out of the nightstand and began reading it for myself. I started with the Gospel of John. Butch wasn't there, but for some reason, I didn't need him. The message was clear. I knew what the next step was.

> We really didn't know it then, but our lives would never be the same.

Sliding off the bed, I knelt to pray. A complete novice at this, I decided to talk to God as though He were next to me. That was the best I could do.

"God, I don't know everything about You. I doubt if I ever will. I'm a sinner and I know I want to be forgiven. I want Christ in my life. I want to become a Christian. I accept You. Amen."

When I opened my eyes, I saw no flashes of light or visions of angels, but somehow I knew this was a big moment. I got back onto the bed and kept reading.

In a while, Butch came back and I nonchalantly told him what I had done. Although I knew he was happy for me, he matter-of-factly told me that I needed to get a Bible of my own and spend time reading it. He also told me that I should look for a good church and find other Christians to hang out with.

My faith was very personal, and it became extremely important to me. I found myself praying a lot, slowly asking God into

> I saw no flashes of light or visions of angels, but somehow I knew this was a big moment.

the details of my life. I found some other players who were Christians, too. And I discovered some great Christian music that encouraged me and lifted my spirits.

My faith brought me stability, an understanding of the big picture, and personal peace. God brought balance.

JOHNNY AND THE HYMN SINGER

The morning after our nerve-racking experience at LAX, I got a call from Freddie DeCordova, the producer of *The Tonight Show.* He invited me to be on the show . . . that night. Jamie and I had watched Johnny Carson many times and being on his show was going to be a thrill. Now I was going *beyond* my wildest dreams.

Little did I know that my three or four minutes on the show would make Johnny's annual "Tonight Show Highlights" anniversary celebration every year until he retired. It was an unforgettable experience.

The show was taped in Los Angeles, so of course the studio audience gave me a big welcome when I was introduced. Johnny congratulated me about my performance in the Series, then he asked about my singing.

"I read something in the paper that when you get a little distressed and you want a little control . . . you sing to yourself." Then he added, "You sing some hymns?"

I began to tell Johnny about the songs and then decided that I might as well show him. I started to sing the Doxology. I figured it was easier to just go ahead and sing rather than to explain what I had been up to during the most intense moments of the

Series. How, sitting on the bench, I would lean my head back against the cement block wall behind me, close my eyes, and sing to myself. The cameras had caught me.

Praise God from whom all blessings flow.
Praise Him all creatures here below.

That night, in front of Johnny Carson and millions of viewers, as I sang the final two lines, my voice cracked with emotion. I closed my eyes as I had in the dugout. A few musicians in the band picked up the tune.

Praise Him above ye heavenly hosts.
Praise Father, Son, and Holy Ghost.

When I finished, the audience erupted in spontaneous applause. "That's very sweet," Johnny said. "That's very sweet." I knew he wasn't being condescending. Johnny and the audience had been touched by the words of the hymn I had first heard twenty years before, standing with Grandpa and Grandma Gillman at the Central Presbyterian Church in Buffalo as the offering plates were brought forward.

Nine years before my appearance with Johnny Carson, Boyd Bartley, the Dodger scout who signed me, had said, "We want you to pitch in Dodger Stadium someday." But if someone had predicted that I would not only pitch at Chavez Ravine, but also win the Cy Young, play for a world champ, win *two* MVP's, and sing the Doxology on *The Tonight Show,* I would have told him he was crazy!

In spite of all of this success and the uncertainties that would follow, God had given me an internal stability and spiritual balance to deal with it. Long-term, that strength proved to be more valuable than anything.

LIVING PEACEFULLY

As I said, everything in our world was being turned upside down. Over the next few months it seemed like the phone rang constantly. Mabel, our housekeeper and nanny, spent much of her time as the family receptionist.

> Long-term, that strength proved to be more valuable than anything.

There was a virtual parade of overnight delivery trucks stopping by our Pasadena home, bringing us stuff we hadn't ordered. Publishers and record companies sent us free books and tapes. Manufacturers of every kind sent us samples, hoping for endorsements. Just a few years before, we never bought anything because we couldn't afford it. Now, packages filled with free things were stacking up in the garage.

We hung on to our old friends and spent as much time with them as we could. But new "friends" came calling. Wondering if people had ulterior motives about being with us wasn't something we'd ever had to think about . . . until now. One night over dinner with a couple who had invited us out, the guy boasted to his wife, "I've always *wanted* a friend who was a Dodger." You and I both know that this guy didn't hang around very long.

During these months, we went through several stages. The first was what Jamie and I had talked about in the noisy van ride from LAX. Because we *were* famous, we were going to be recognized and interrupted. There was nothing we could do about it. Second, we experienced a temptation to hide—to become reclusive. Finally, we wondered if we should carefully ease forward and try to maintain normal lives. We decided to do it.

To help us in this, Jamie and I set boundaries. We learned to say no without feeling guilty. And we stayed involved in our church and continued attending a Bible study with a few couples. Although we were tempted to stay home, we ventured out—going to restaurants, shopping malls, and movies. Facing eager fans who interrupted us was sometimes frustrating, but it was much better than hiding.

I tried to be gracious with being recognized almost everywhere, even when I didn't want to be. Like the time when I was driving on the Pasadena Freeway . . .

DIGGING FOR GOLD IN STYLE

From the time I was a teenager, I had wanted to own a Jaguar . . . a black one . . . a convertible. For years—long before owning one was even a remote possibility—I'd see them on the road and say to myself, *Some day I'm going to have one of those!*

Soon after winning the World Series, I got a check for fifty thousand dollars from Walt Disney. Actually, it was sent to me because I had answered a question as I walked toward the dugout in Oakland. "Hey, Orel," a woman with a microphone had said. "Now that you've won the World Series, what are you going to do?"

"I'm going to Disneyland," I'd answered. The fifty-thousand-dollar check had been a thank-you for saying these words. (Actually, Disney hosted Jamie, the boys, and me the next week. We had a wonderful time.)

Facing eager fans who interrupted us was sometimes frustrating, but it was much better than hiding.

With that money in the bank, I walked into the Jaguar dealer in Pasadena . . . and there it was: "my" black Jag convertible. I paid cash and drove off the lot one very happy man.

A couple months later, I was headed toward Dodger Stadium on the 110—the Pasadena Freeway—in the center lane. It was one of those perfect Southern California days, not a cloud in the sky. I had the top down and the radio turned way up. Whitney Houston was wailing, "One Moment in Time," and I was singing along at the top of my lungs. And, like you sometimes see people do in traffic, I was also picking my nose. Really diggin' for gold.

Something told me I wasn't alone. I looked to my right. Sure enough, there was a guy driving right next to me. "Hey, Bulldog," he said, pumping his fist in the air. I couldn't hear him but I could read his lips. Then he put his finger next to his nose with a big smile and a hey-this-is-cool look on his face.

Completely embarrassed, I turned away.

But next to me, on the left, was another car. Inside was a guy who pumped his fist in the air and shouted, "Hey, Bulldog." Then, exactly like the other guy, he stuck his finger by his nose and gave me a big smile.

I slowed my car down to a crawl and watched the two cars disappear ahead of me around the next turn. So much for venturing out. At that moment, isolation was looking pretty good again.

Living in the public eye was a new challenge. But we wanted to live as normally as possible. Balance was the goal. We hung onto our faith; we stayed in close contact with our old friends; we didn't hide; and we tried to keep our sense of humor. A good lesson in balance.

Over the years, there were lots of other important lessons about balance to be learned.

BALANCING DIRECTNESS AND DIPLOMACY

One of the things you get accustomed to as a professional athlete is conversational bluntness. Your coaches, the trainers, and your teammates aren't worried about being tactful. Advice is delivered without regard. Abrupt words come with the territory.

On visits to the mound, coaches have no time for diplomacy. Not only are there time constraints enforced by an umpire, but coaches have something important to say and they're going to go ahead and say it. There's no reason to hold anything back.

What a waste of time it would have been if, during my rehab from shoulder reconstruction, Pat Screnar had looked for the appropriate moment, then hinted about what he thought I should do. During those months, even when I felt defeated and my attitude was miserable, Pat stuck to his plan. Frankly, he didn't seem to care what my response was to his assignment for me on any given day; he told me what to do and he expected me to follow through.

> One of the things you get accustomed to as a professional athlete is conversational bluntness.

Players are no exception to the bluntness rule. Once when I was with the Mets, one of our best hitters stepped into the batter's box with one out and a runner at third. It was an important moment in the game. After working the pitcher to a full count, he popped up to the shortstop. For some guys, hitting a pop-up is worse than striking out, especially in a situation where a solid fly ball would have scored a run. He came back to the dugout, fuming at what had just happened. Ripping off his batting helmet and gloves and tossing them aside, he plopped down on the bench. No one spoke to him.

Now with two outs, Robin Ventura, the next batter, settled in. Not only did he get a base hit and bring the man home from third; he ripped a dinger over the right field fence for a two-run homer. We were ecstatic. Most of the guys jumped out of the dugout to welcome him home. Meanwhile our friend, Mr. Pop-up, didn't move. In fact, when Robin stepped down into the dugout and walked past him, he didn't lift his hand for a high five. Mr. Pop-up's eyes were glued to the floor.

"Hey, man, that's straight jealousy," Robin chided with a

smile on his face, loud enough for plenty of guys to hear. Mr. Pop-up looked up, shooting an eyeful at Robin. Everyone laughed. In a moment, Mr. Pop-up joined in. Like I said, brutal frankness is part of the game and Robin Ventura had a knack for it.

In baseball, the direct approach is pretty effective. But in life this kind of candor has the potential of creating all kinds of problems. Several years ago, some of our friends gave me the nickname "Dr. Stiletto." I guess they had noticed the way I didn't hold back from cutting straight to the point—speaking my mind. Baseball had taught me well, although this attribute wasn't something I was always proud of.

I had a lot to learn, jumping from one world to the other. Tact in baseball is not standard fare. But outside the game, I had some work to do. At one end of the spectrum is directness, and at the other end is diplomacy. The object is to live somewhere between the two.

Several years ago, some of our friends gave me the nickname "Dr. Stiletto."

My challenge was being brave enough to say something about the "elephant in the room" with compassion and the good of the other person in mind. It was speaking honestly without being hurtful.

This meant that before I spoke the truth, I needed to work on having a gentle spirit toward the person I was speaking to. For example, I knew that Pat Screnar truly cared for me. That was a given. So I was able to accept his directness because I trusted his motives.

Directness *and* diplomacy are important in every relationship, but nowhere is this more important than in my life as a husband and a father. Do I love my family enough to tell them the truth? Of course. But what about timing? What about causing unnecessary embarrassment for my wife or sons because I've blurted

> Directness *and* diplomacy are important in every relationship, but nowhere is this more important than in my life as a husband and a father.

something out at the wrong moment? When I've done this, the point I was trying to make has gotten lost in the hurt and I've had to apologize.

Even tough-love—speaking the truth to someone I love—must be tempered with care and good timing.

Dr. Stiletto meets Mr. Discretion.

BALANCING THE FUTURE AND THE PRESENT

A raging river is actually just a swamp with boundaries. A life that's lived without order is stagnant and useless. During my years as a professional athlete, I had the reputation of being intentional about my work—having a plan when I walked onto the field.

It's true. From my early years in the majors, I looked for success formulas and sometimes banked them before I needed to use them. Collecting wasn't a new thing for me. Having learned the value of accumulating stamps and coins from my grandpa and my dad, this was a familiar path. Now my baseball collection was more than just cards; it was good habits, techniques, and approaches to the game that I saw in other players.

Because I saw veterans who didn't seem to have good stuff on the mound but were winning, I learned that "smart" and "ready" would be as valuable to me as "athletic" and "talented." This plan was a constant companion. It was born from my respect for my teammates and opponents and it continued throughout my career.

But my planning wasn't only about the future. I know this may sound a little eccentric, but each time I walked to the mound I had a mental checklist. It was thorough and very detailed. And even before I stepped onto the field, my pregame regimen—rubdown from the trainer, stretching, warm-ups, studying the opposing team's lineup, the way I put my uniform on—had been meticulously orchestrated. Like an airline pilot going down his preflight index of details, I reviewed the checklist:

- my posture on the mound
- the weight distribution on my feet
- the length of my step back
- the height and aggressiveness of my leg kick
- the first movement toward the plate
- the focus of my eyes
- the finish of the pitch
- the follow through

It may sound crazy that even after years and years of pitching, I still relied on the basics. I knew that success was often an invitation to forget planning and self-examination. But imbedded in my thinking was the absolute necessity of having an immediate plan when I went to the mound. Without it I could have become distracted and unfocused.

Then, depending on my own condition that day and the strengths and weaknesses of the hitter I was facing, I made adjustments. In key situations I checked the position of my infielders and outfielders. Everyone needed to be on the same page. Should they shift left or right? Should they back up or draw in?

Success was often an invitation to forget planning and self-examination.

Knowing there would be

constant surprises, I had a future and a present plan. This plan brought a calm, a readiness, and a security.

DISTRACTIONS TO THE PLAN

Has my concentration on this plan ever been interrupted? Yes, of course. It happened all the time.

In the summer of 1985, we had a four-game home series against San Diego. The day before my start, I was playing with our son Quinton in our bedroom. With no warning, he jumped off the bed and broke his collarbone. I felt terrible. We spent the day in the emergency room. A social worker subtly interrogated Jamie and me separately, asking leading questions about possible child abuse. This upset me even more.

When I walked to the mound the next day in San Diego, my mind was somewhere else.

Before I knew it, Tim Flannery had lined a lead-off single to left and Garry Templeton, the second hitter, had singled through the infield. Then I got Tony Gwynn to ground into a force out. The next batter, Craig Nettles, delivered a wake-up call with a bullet off the right field fence for a double.

I stepped off the back of the mound and gave the Bulldog a serious lecture. *Wait a minute, dummy*, I rebuked myself. *You can't be thinking about Quinton out here. Either pitch this game or get off the mound and go home. You can take care of him later.*

I checked back in—or I should say I checked in for the *first* time—and decided to stay and play. Quinton was in Jamie's capable hands. I'd be home soon enough.

Stepping back onto the mound, I scanned my checklist. I reviewed the situation, recommitting myself to the plan. We won 7-1.

Three years later, right in the middle of the fifty-nine scoreless innings streak and a serious pennant race, our son Jordan was born. As he was being delivered, baby Jordan aspirated some

Stepping back onto the mound, I scanned my checklist. I reviewed the situation, recommitting myself to the plan.

amniotic fluid, filling his lungs with liquid. It nearly strangled him. Jordan was put in intensive care and for the moment our lives stood still.

I had a start coming up against the Astros and Tommy left the decision up to me—whether to travel to Houston or stay in Los Angeles with Jamie and Jordan and catch up with the team later. I didn't want to leave. But the next day Jordan improved, so the doctors moved him from intensive to intermediate care. Jamie encouraged me to fly to Houston and I made my start.

I remember walking to the mound that night in the Astrodome to start the game. I had a choice: be distracted by what I could not control back in Los Angeles or commit to the task at hand. I chose the latter. At the end of the evening, I had thrown another shutout and my scoreless inning streak had reached forty.

Many sports reporters and writers have speculated about what makes an average major leaguer into a standout—a star into a legend. I've thought about this, too.

If you were to visit any major league clubhouse, you'd find gifted athletes. There's no question about it; these men are very, very good at what they do. The odds are so strongly stacked against them even making it to this level that you *know* they're very special. Every one of them.

These guys can steal a base, execute a sacrifice bunt, scoop up a ground ball and fire it over to first in time for the out. They can beat out a slow roller to third for a base hit. They can hit a home run.

But less than 1 percent of these men will make it to the Hall of Fame.

Of course, there is no guaranteed road to Cooperstown, but if a player has a chance of getting there, he must have a plan. A strategy that not only includes doing those things I just mentioned every once in a while, but a goal to get on base *every time* he's up to bat, even if it means running his guts out when it looks like he's hit a routine ground ball to an infielder. A goal to steal a base *every time* he gets on by studying the pitching motion of the man on the mound. A goal to advance runners and, if possible, bring them home to score. And a goal to play errorless ball by remembering his checklist of fundamentals and mechanics.

Someone once said if you fail to plan, you plan to fail. This is certainly true in baseball.

Even though I only reached base once in every five tries, I had *planned* to reach base every single time. Even though I never hit a home run (I had one triple in 1988 and another one in 1989) I *tried* to swing for the fence more times than you could know. Even though I injured myself more than once trying to beat out a grounder, it didn't matter. I wanted to do everything I could to get on base.

Even though I was on base over 160 times and only stole eight bases, I studied the pitching motion of my opponent and looked for a chance to steal, every time. Even though I had fifty runs batted in (RBIs), which was excellent for a pitcher, I planned to advance runners every time I had a chance. And even though my fielding was known for its accuracy, I was never complacent about committing an error. My plan was errorless fielding.

You may wonder if I'm boasting by saying all of these things. Actually, I'm doing the opposite. I'm reminding both of us that I failed more times than I succeeded. Even though my preparation and my intensity were as focused as I could make them, I was unsuccessful at execution more than I was successful. But it was always my conscious intention to succeed. My strategy was to examine the checklist and execute.

And whether you or I ever make our respective Halls of Fame, this is something we both can do.

As you'll see in the next chapter, I love spontaneity. Surprises and last minute ideas can be a great adventure. But without a plan, impulsiveness produces chaos.

Spontaneity has to be balanced with order. Intensity and creativity must live inside a plan.

> Even though my preparation and my intensity were as focused as I could make them, I was unsuccessful at execution more than I was successful.

BALANCING BASEBALL AND REAL LIFE

During the season, with all its intricate twists and turns of workout regimens, starts, and travel, it was easy to live in a cocoon. With no effort at all, I could shut the rest of the world out and live from day to day with no perspective . . . no balance.

Thankfully, Jamie saw to it that this didn't happen. Even though it meant expending an incredible amount of energy and creativity, she did her best to make sure that I didn't lose contact with my family and my friends.

During my years in Cleveland, San Francisco, and New York, and when I returned to Los Angeles in 2000, she rented places for our family to live. Just as soon as school was out, she and the boys would literally move to these places and she would do her very best to turn these rental houses or apartments into "home." She knew that, although baseball was my career, I had to balance it with life as a husband, dad, and friend. So she orchestrated all the details to give me a home during those years.

At the beginning of each season, Jamie would sit down with

my road-trip schedule and a calendar. She would do her very best to make sure that I didn't have more than a week without a visit from her, from our sons, from my siblings or parents, or from a few of my closest friends. Instead of hanging out in lonely hotel rooms day after day, these visits from family and friends created some of the fondest memories of my twenty-one years in the game.

Jamie's creativity gave me a life outside of baseball, even during the most intense seasons. It was a taste of real life and it was necessary; it provided me balance, and it was wonderful.

BECOMING A BALANCED PERSON

What does a person have to do to be given the title "The World's Fastest Man"?

I'm not sure who established this tradition, but the answer is to be the active athlete who holds the world's record in the hundred-meter dash. Over the years names like Jesse Owens ('36), Carl Lewis ('84 and '88), and Maurice Greene (2000), made the headlines: The World's Fastest Man.

But who holds the designation "The World's Greatest Athlete"?

Again, I don't know who made the rule, but this title is given to the athlete who wins the decathlon every four years at the Summer Olympics: memorable athletes like Bob Mathias ('48, '52), Rafer Johnson ('60), and Bruce Jenner ('76).

Why is this man given this title? Actually, it usually *isn't*

Instead of hanging out in lonely hotel rooms day after day, these visits from family and friends created some of the fondest memories of my twenty-one years in the game.

because he's the world's best at any of the ten events he competes in. In fact, before he won the decathlon in the 1976 Montreal Games, Bruce Jenner trained for four years with the world-record holder in each of the ten events. That meant that he did nothing but *lose* all those races, throws, and jumps for four years.

But by putting them all together, he became the world's greatest athlete because he was "The World's Most Balanced Athlete."

As you understand that God loves you whether you're winning or losing—that's balance. As you learn to speak the truth with love—that's balance. As you commit yourself to a plan that includes the future and the present—that's balance. And as you keep a strong perspective on the difference between your work and your life—that's balance.

You may not be a world record holder at anything, but you can still be a great champion. The key is to live in balance.

PRINCIPLE #6

Ability to Lighten Up

Most baseball fans have seen my intensity on the playing field. My game face and attitude have been well documented.

But off the field, I was a very different person. I loved to laugh.

BASEBALL'S BORDER WARS

Almost every battle ever fought began with a dispute over land. Some of history's greatest conflicts started with arguments about borders and boundaries . . . like the celebrated war between the Hatfields and the McCoys.

Do you remember the feuds between these two rural families? Most of the skirmishes were over the property line drawn between their farms.

The dispute in baseball between the pitcher and the hitter is exactly the same. It's all about real estate—what's yours and what's mine. As I saw it, the outer half of the strike zone was my land and the inner half was the batter's. Leaning over the prop-

I loved to laugh.

erty line into my land represented too much comfort, plate coverage, and visibility for the hitter. Encroaching on my territory gave him an unfair advantage. This was not good. When the hitter tried to turn the outside corner into the middle of the plate, it was time to go to the gun cabinet.

Wandering onto my land was built into a hitter's psyche, so I would simply show him the copy of my deed and enforce my zoning laws. If not, my land—and my livelihood—would be gone.

Pitchers call these *purpose pitches*. And the expectation is that the batter will get back on his personal real estate . . . in a hurry . . . maybe sitting on his butt as he returns. This is the only way a pitcher can politely ask the hitter to back up.

If you want proof beyond my own claim that I never *intentionally* hit a batter, would it help if I mentioned that a player never charged the mound after being hit by me? Not once. Okay, a few started toward me and stopped. Who knows why, but I hope they all realized that I never deliberately tried to hurt them. Come to think of it, maybe they felt sorry for the skinny guy on the mound. They had learned on the playground to never fight someone who looked like me.

Either way, no batter ever retaliated . . . except for a few choice words as the guy took his base.

Okay, so there was *one* situation where a batter charged me . . . ten years later. Let me explain.

A LITTLE BROTHERLY LOVE

It was August 1998. I was with the Giants and we were playing a three-game weekend series with the Phillies. It was one of those muggy Sunday afternoons and, as it turned out, tempers were about as hot.

I had started the day before, so I was watching the game from the dugout.

We were batting in the top of the fifth inning with a five-run lead. Barry Bonds stepped up to the plate having already logged two hits and a walk for the day. He promptly lined a single into right field.

Barry took a big lead off first and, as soon as he had a chance, stole second base.

There's an unwritten rule in baseball that when a team has a commanding lead and it's late in the game, that team doesn't do things to run up the score—like sacrifice bunts or stealing bases. Winning is one thing; humiliating your opponent is another. With that steal and a five-run lead—although it was only the fifth inning—some of the guys on the Phillies' bench were a little upset with Barry.

> Okay, so there was *one* situation where a batter charged me . . . ten years later. Let me explain.

I'm sure the fact that it was Barry and this was his third hit of the afternoon just made things worse.

Two innings later, Barry came to the plate again. Terry Francona, the Phillies' manager, called time-out and walked to the mound. Looking to the bullpen he signaled for Matt Whiteside to come in and face Barry. Mike Lieberthal, the Phillies' catcher, joined Francona on the mound. We were a little surprised to see Whiteside, since he had pitched three full innings the day before. Most relievers get more than one day's rest after seeing that much action.

Once Whiteside had reached the mound, Francona had a few words with him, handed him the ball, and trotted to the Phillies' dugout. Lieberthal walked back to his position behind home plate.

Scroll ahead a few hours.

I was standing in front of a video monitor in the visitor's clubhouse after the game. Mark "Gardy" Gardner, one of my fellow Giant starters, was running the machine. Barry was standing next to me and we were watching the replay of the moment Whiteside got to the mound to face him.

> "You hit me," I repeated. "You know, we *are* on the same team now!"

As Whiteside readied himself on the mound and looked in for the sign from Lieberthal, Gardy noticed something on the tape. Actually, there was something he *didn't* notice. He rewound the video and played it again. "Look, there's no sign," Gardy shouted. "Leiberthal didn't give Whiteside a sign."

Sure enough, as we looked at it again, there was no sign—no signal telling Whiteside what to throw. Our guess was that Leiberthal, Francona, and Whiteside had decided what he was going to do when they met on the mound.

The first and only pitch Whiteside had thrown was a fastball right at Barry. He tried to jump out of the way but the ball hit him squarely in the thigh. Barry did not hesitate for a moment. Dropping his bat, he charged the mound at full speed. Whiteside braced himself; Barry has the physique of a linebacker—not someone you'd want to tangle with under any circumstances.

Both benches emptied. I was one of the last ones out of the dugout and slowly circled the battle in the center of the infield, looking for one-on-one fights I thought I could break up.

In a few minutes the fight ended. Barry was ejected from the game, along with Matt Whiteside and Terry Francona. I guess the umpires saw what we saw.

After the game, as I stood in the clubhouse watching the video with Barry and Gardy, Danny Darwin walked past. "Whatcha up to?" he said to me in his Texas-cowboy twang.

Danny was a veteran pitcher—the only guy on the team who

was older than me. When I looked at him I could tell he was up to something.

And then I remembered. During the melee on the mound I had taken a few errant shots.

"Hey, you hit me today," I said to Danny, who just stood there smiling. "You unloaded on my arm in that fight. You hit me," I repeated. "You know, we *are* on the same team now!"

Danny didn't deny it. Nor did he stop smiling. He told me that ten years before, when he was a starter with Houston and I was with the Dodgers, I had thrown him some "chin music"—one of those purpose pitches. The ball hadn't actually hit him but he had eaten some dirt getting out of the way.

Danny had been looking for a chance to get me back for a long, long time. He turned and walked away, cracking up all the way back to his locker. I couldn't believe it but I laughed right along with him.

LAUGHTER IS THE BEST ROUTINE

During that same year with the Giants, I played with Steve "Reeder" Reed, one of our relievers. Reeder had an unbelievable sense of humor and he kept a lot of us off balance in the clubhouse.

Because the players arrived at the ballpark at different times, Stan Conte, the team's physical therapist, would put workout assignments—especially for starting pitchers—on a chalkboard just inside the door to the workout room. A typical chart would look like this:

Estes	Cardio for 20	Heavy lower body	Stretch	Arm weights
Gardner	Lower body	Upper body	Cardio for 45	Stretch
Hershiser	Abs	Cardio for 45	Stretch	Lower body
Reed	Upper body	Arm weights	Abs	Stretch

Putting the workouts on the board not only told us what Stan wanted us to do, but it also gave us a chance to see what other guys were doing so we could possibly hook up with them.

But sometimes, when I'd walk past the chalkboard, I'd find something like this.

Estes	Cardio for 20	Heavy lower body	Stretch	Arm weights
Gardner	Lower body	Upper body	Cardio for 45	Stretch
Hershiser	Sign autographs	Eat	Interviews	Take nap
Reed	Upper body	Arm weights	Abs	Stretch

I knew Reeder was behind this. After Stan wrote my workout, Reeder would sneak to the board when no one was looking and make his own adjustments to my schedule. I'd let it ride so he could enjoy all the mileage from his creativity. Another one of the unwritten rules in ball is that you're not supposed to disarm a prank until most have enjoyed it. Even if it's at your own expense.

DUGOUT ANTICS

My first year with Cleveland was awesome. I had never played with a team so overpowering. The cumulative batting average of the starters was .294, a great thing for every pitcher on the team. I always loved being the beneficiary of a great offense. That year I learned to live with 8.4 runs per game. The offense did its thing and we finished the year with one hundred wins, thrilling Cleveland fans who filled Jacobs Field to capacity for every home game.

To say that this team was "loose" would be an understatement. Sitting in the dugout during a game, I was privy to some hilarious moments. When one of our teammates would strike out in a situation that wasn't critical and awkwardly fall down, the guys would bury him when he'd return to the dugout. "Are you okay?" someone would crack. "Good thing you fell down. I think I see the sniper up there," pointing to the stands. There would be laughs everywhere—including the guy who had just embarrassed himself.

Or when someone would trip and fall on the base paths, one of the guys would act like he was calling the grounds crew. "Get down here and rake those dangerous craters out of the way. Someone's gonna get hurt."

Sometimes one of the guys who was working his gum—Alvaro Espinoza and Wayne Kirby were the best at this—would blow a big bubble. They'd take it and quietly stick it to the button on top of someone's hat. The rest of the players in the dugout would try to keep from making their laughter too obvious so the victim would run out onto the field at the end of the inning, his bubble firmly in place.

Once he was out of the dugout, we'd let loose and really laugh.

But whatever fun we had playing tricks on our teammates that season, it didn't compare to the fun we had pounding our opponents.

A RECORD-BREAKING STREAK

Roger McDowell was one of my favorite teammates. If he hadn't been blessed with a great arm, he could have been a stand-up comic. Roger was with the Dodgers during my first few years back from shoulder reconstruction. His antics may have sped up the healing process.

> "Get down here and rake those dangerous craters out of the way. Someone's gonna get hurt."

"Bizarre" or "off-the-wall" described this guy to a tee.

One of Roger's goals was to see how many ballparks he could shag in . . . naked. As many cities as possible, completely naked. (I'm laughing out loud just thinking about it.)

Of course, this was done during early BP when no fans were allowed into the park. At around 2:30 P.M., Roger would walk out onto the field with his glove. He'd be wearing tennis shoes, a tee shirt, and a loose pair of shorts. That was it.

As the fly balls were hit to the outfield, Roger would kick off his tennis shoes. Then the shirt would follow. Just at the right moment, when the next ball was headed his way, he'd rip off his shorts and capture one in the buff.

His ultimate goal was to do this in every major-league yard. I'm not sure how close he got, but when he retired, I think he had only missed a few.

AN EXCEPTION

What I've said about pitching coaches carefully watching their pitchers is true. The fact that they'll stride to the mound to give strategic advice or to ask if you are too tired to continue is usually true. "Usually" is the operative word here.

Ron "Perry" Perranoski was my pitching coach during most of my years with the Dodgers. He was an excellent coach who knew how to get the most from his pitchers. During one outing at Wrigley Field, Perry called time-out and walked to the mound. I thought everything I was doing was in synch, so I was surprised to see him coming out. *What's he coming out here for?* I remember thinking to myself. *A guy on second with two outs—this is not that big a deal.*

Perry stood facing me with his back to home plate.

"Look over the dugout," were his first words.

I obeyed, still having no idea what he was up to.

"Do you see June? Look carefully."

I scanned the area above the dugout, looking for his wife. "I don't see her," I said. "Why do you want me to look for her?"

"We bought an Illinois lottery ticket. The numbers have been drawn. It's worth millions. She told me that if we won, she would come to the game and stand behind the dugout during my first visit to the mound. That was our signal. I told her that if I saw her, I'd take my uniform top off right here on the mound, walk to the dugout, and retire."

> Just at the right moment, when the next ball was headed his way, he'd rip off his shorts and capture one in the buff.

He smiled at me. "Then you'd be on your own, pal."

A moment of silence passed. "I guess this means I'll be around," Perry grumbled. He turned and walked back to the dugout while I shook my head in disbelief.

The next hitter grounded out and the inning was over. Back on the bench, I overheard Perry explaining to Tommy how his great advice had made the difference.

BAD TIMING

Sometimes attempts at humor were poorly timed. Often these moments came from guys who tended to be more reserved but who would occasionally do something crazy. Take Jesse Orosco, for example.

Needing a left-handed reliever, the Dodgers acquired Jesse from the Mets in 1988. He was a great guy. Fun-loving—but not a comedian. Jesse joined us for his first Dodger Spring Training in Vero Beach. As we were dressing for the first game, the atmosphere in the clubhouse was pretty light. Guys were jabbing each other about weight they had gained in the off-season or the speckled boxer shorts someone had gotten from his wife.

For some reason, Jesse took a stab at doing something he thought would be funny. Maybe he was trying to work his way into a new situation. He took one of the player's caps and, along the inside rim, smeared some eye black. Great prank, but I think Jesse needed to do a little more research on his victim. He would have found out that, although Kirk Gibson was fun loving, game time was no time to be messing with him.

> Back on the bench, I overheard Perry explaining to Tommy how his great advice had made the difference.

Once we got to the field, Kirk pulled his cap off to run his wind sprints. There, across his forehead for all the world to see, was a huge black streak. Someone made a crack, which set Gibby off. He was furious.

"That's it," he barked as he headed for the clubhouse. "I'm done. I'm out of here. Trade me."

We didn't see him again the rest of the day. He just took off. He didn't play in the game. We had no idea where he went. I don't know this for sure, but my guess is that Jesse didn't get much sleep that night.

The next morning, Gibby called a team meeting. I looked over at Jesse sitting in front of his locker. He looked terrible. Gibby made no bones about the fact that he was going to crush whoever had done this to him. The tension was pretty thick. We knew Gibby wasn't kidding. Except for Kirk Gibson himself, everyone knew exactly who had done this, but no one said a thing.

Fortunately, in a day or two, Gibby got over it. And eventually Jesse fessed up to the now infamous crime. Lucky for Jesse, enough time had passed and Gibby eventually calmed down and let Jesse off the hook.

FUN WITH THE SKIPPER

In baseball, no one is off limits when it comes to clubhouse banter. There's a pecking order. Managers and coaches can pick on veterans. Veterans can pick on rookies, rookies can pick on clubhouse staff, and anyone can pick on reporters and strangers. But all who dare return the teasing back *up* the line dish it out at their own risk. Some coaches and managers keep a subtle but firm lid on ribbing from their players. But during my years with the Dodgers, it sure wasn't the case.

"If Tommy was two inches shorter, he'd be a perfect circle."

This was—and is—Tommy Lasorda. Manager? Yeah. Instigator? For sure. Target? Of course.

"That's it," he barked as he headed for the clubhouse. "I'm done. I'm out of here. Trade me."

Tommy gave it to us and was a good sport about getting it back. Someone—Steve Sax often did this—would act like he had a microphone in his hand, doing stand-up comedy.

"As you can see," Saxy would say, rolling his eyes, "Tommy started working out in the off-season. He was using a rowing machine, but he had to quit. It sank."

"If Tommy was two inches shorter, he'd be a perfect circle."

"In Spring Training, Tommy gave us two choices for running. It was either three times around the field or twice around him."

Saxy was on a roll.

Not every manager could take this. But Tommy was a magician at bringing his team together. Tommy Lasorda wasn't "every manager."

THE SOD SQUAD

One year, the Dodgers were having a tough time playing on AstroTurf. Our record on grass was terrific, but on the fake stuff we were miserable.

One afternoon as I was walking to the bullpen in right field, I noticed an area where the grounds crew kept spare turf growing. The proverbial lightbulb came on in my head.

Without telling anyone, I got a shovel and dug up a few strips of the grass, stuffed them in a big, empty duffel bag, and put it on the plane for our next trip to Pittsburgh.

> "Okay, you guys. This stuff is from Dodger Stadium. You've got no excuses now."

Just before the game with the Pirates, as my teammates were doing their last minute warm-ups on the field, I loaded the sod—about five big pieces—into a grocery cart and wheeled it down the tunnel to the dugout. I set all the gloves and towels and things aside, carefully laying the sod on the floor of the dugout. Then I laid their gloves and things back on the sod.

When everybody came back to the dugout they were mystified. "Hey, what's this?" "What's the grass for?" "Who did this?"

I spoke up. "Okay, you guys. This stuff is from Dodger Stadium. You've got no excuses now."

"Aw c'mon," they said. "What kind of an idiot would do something like this?"

But we won that first game on Three Rivers Stadium's AstroTurf. So the grass stayed in the dugout for the series. And you guessed it—we took it with us for the next series at Veteran's Stadium in Philly.

A couple of guys joined me in taking care of the grass. We watered it and even asked the groundskeepers in the stadiums if we could borrow some fertilizer. (You should have seen their faces.) The wins kept coming and the press took notice. On the road we became "The Sod Squad."

By the end of the trip, the grass was looking pretty shabby so before we left for the next series on AstroTurf, we replaced it with some new pieces from Dodger Stadium.

Hey, it was a dirty job, but someone had to do it.

"AREN'T YOU OREL HERSHISER?"

It was one thing for me to be recognized at a restaurant or a shopping mall, but being pointed out in public men's rooms was another thing altogether. The call of nature is, of course, one thing we all have in common—even professional athletes. And when it calls, there's no hanging up.

At sporting events—other than my own—there were occasionally men in these facilities who had consumed too much of their favorite beverage. Time, volume, and velocity were major clues.

"Hey, Bulldog," one would shout after recognizing me.

"How ya doin', Orel?" someone else would bellow, loud enough for everyone to hear.

Now all the men and boys in the bathroom would be staring at me.

"Hey, that's Hershiser over there," someone would screech.

"Hey, that's Hershiser over there," someone would screech.

"Yeah, it is," his buddy would add. "Go, Dodgers."

Then, to top it off, once I had finished and was heading for the sinks to wash up, all these guys would want to shake my hand . . . before they'd had a chance to wash their hands. Watching me dance around the men's room trying to avoid these handshakes was an exercise in itself.

By the way, the next time you catch me in one of those situations, don't think I'm being rude if I just smile and wave.

NOT TOO GREAT ON DIRECTIONS

People who know me know that I am directionally challenged. I've actually gotten lost just a few miles from my own home. In fact, I bought my last car primarily for the on-board Global Positioning System (GPS). That in-dash computer screen has helped me find my way many a time.

A few years ago, during the off-season, Jamie and I took the boys to one of our favorite beach hotels for a few days of R and R. I quietly made arrangements for a deep-sea fishing expedition with the boys. The night before, I told them that early the next day we were going to give Jamie the morning to relax and go on a surprise adventure. I carefully memorized the directions from the hotel to the dock where we were to meet our fishing boat. I had the directions down. I wasn't going to get lost.

As we went down the elevator the next morning, the boys hammered me with questions.

"Where are we going, Dad?"

I held my ground.

"Are you sure you know how to get there?"

I promised them that I did.

"Yeah, sure, Dad." They'd been lost with me too many times.

The valet had our car waiting in front of the hotel. Holding the door open for me, he asked the inevitable. "Mr. Hershiser, do you need any help with directions?"

I handed him a tip, confidently assuring him that no directions would be necessary this morning. The boys got into the car without saying anything.

We pulled away from the hotel, ready for some fun. But in just a few hundred yards—still on hotel property—I was faced with a fork in the road. Going left looked like it led back to the hotel. Right was surely the way to the main road.

I eased right and hit the gas.

In seconds we were looping back under the hotel into the parking garage. The boys were laughing their heads off. And the only way out was to drive through the garage and across the front of the hotel again. I smiled at the valet as I drove past.

"'Mr. Hershiser, do you need any help with directions?'" Quinton jabbed from the backseat.

"No, thank you," I laughed.

LET A SMILE BE YOUR UMBRELLA

Your life may already be filled with plenty of laughter. That's good. If not, "Lighten up!" may be the prescription you need. Look for the joy in life and enjoy the laughter everywhere you can.

PRINCIPLE #7

Love Your Family

You already know how important my coaches have been to me. Their advice shaped me into the athlete I turned out to be. You also know that not all of my coaches have been those who have given me tips about baseball. One of my greatest coaches was my sports representative. The counsel he gave me about my priorities and my family is something I'll never forget.

I met Robert Fraley during my first Spring Training with the Dodgers in 1984. He had made the short trip from his home in Orlando to Vero Beach to meet with me and to discuss the possibility of his firm representing me.

I remember being impressed with Robert's intelligence, his warmth, and his understated class. I also loved his dry sense of humor and his unmistakable integrity and faith. Soon I signed with his firm, Leader Enterprises.

During those first few years in the majors, Robert kept all my contracts and professional relationships in order. In 1988, my career took off. I finished the season having broken Don Drysdale's record by pitching fifty-nine consecutive scoreless innings. I had helped the underrated Dodgers to the National League pennant and had been named the Most Valuable Player of the NLCS. Then, facing the Oakland A's, I again assisted the Dodgers in victory, winning two games and being named the Most Valuable Player of the World Series.

Sports Illustrated put me on their cover and awarded me their Sportsman of the Year and *The Sporting News* named me Major League Player of the Year. The National League gave me the highest honor for a pitcher—the Cy Young—and the Associated Press honored me as the Professional Athlete of the Year. I also won a Gold Glove for being the best fielder in my position.

The phone in Robert's office started lighting up. Proposals for endorsements came flooding in. Book offers were made. I was besieged with interview requests. There was talk that I would be offered a contract, making me the highest-paid baseball player in history. And in November it came true. The Red Sox had just presented Roger Clemens with a three-year deal for $7.5 million then the Dodgers came to the table with a $7.9 million contract for me.

I'll admit that this was an overwhelming experience.

It had always been Robert's goal to get the best contract for me. His professional skills were impeccable. And when he was negotiating on my behalf, I felt completely confident. But Robert was more than just a gifted attorney and complete gentleman. He was a man of unwavering character with wisdom beyond his years.

The numbers didn't impress Robert. He knew there was more to life than this. "You're at the top of your game, Orel, and you're about to make a lot of money. But that is not true success."

Robert spoke the truth in a way that was never condescending. And he often spoke with a hint of a smile on his face.

"Success will be measured at the end of your career, not at the peak," he said. "When you're finished with baseball, if you love God, if you're still in love with your wife, if your children know who you are, and if your reputation is still intact, then you'll be successful."

"When you're finished with baseball, if you love God, if you're still in love with your wife, if your children know who you are, and if your reputation is still intact, then you'll be successful."

Robert was right. I didn't want my success to come at the expense of my family—to allow fame and fortune to jeopardize my goal of reaching the peak in my personal life, too.

Like my coaches coming to the mound and telling me the truth, Robert Fraley's words had set a new standard. And this new standard was about the things most dear to me: my faith and my family. I had done all I could to try to be the best pitcher in the game. This was a challenge to keep me from forgetting my priorities or slacking off about being successful in life.

Robert's words were a great gift to me.

ACROSS A CROWDED ROOM

When I met her during the summer of 1980, Jamie Byars had just graduated summa cum laude from the University of Iowa with a degree in Vocal Performance. She was planning to attend graduate school but was taking a year off to study voice privately while living with her parents in San Antonio.

Jamie's dad, Douglas Byars, was an executive with Sigmor Corporation, a company owned and run by Mr. Tom Turner. Mr. Turner also owned the Double A San Antonio Dodgers. I was playing for San Antonio and we were having a terrific season, sitting on top of our division halfway through the summer. In June Mr. Turner threw a celebration party for the team at his home and also invited his company's senior executives.

Unfortunately, Mr. Byars was going to be out of town so he asked Jamie to escort her mom to the party.

With all due respect to the above-average intelligence of professional athletes, Jamie told her mother that the last thing she wanted to do was to go to a party to meet "a bunch of dumb jocks." But because she could tell that her mother really wanted to go, Jamie agreed to accompany her.

And I am so glad she did.

As though it were last week, I can clearly remember the first time I saw her. Even though there were about 250 people at the party, she definitely caught my eye. And I guess that there was something about me that caught her crystal blue eyes, too. During the evening, we made visual contact a number of times. We also checked each other out during trips to the buffet table, especially at the Shrimp Paesano. I smiled at her and was pretty sure she returned my smile.

The Turners had a huge family room, complete with three television sets. When the ten o'clock news came on, I walked over to see what was going on in the world. Because there were lots of people watching the three screens, there was no place to sit. As I stood toward the back of the room watching ABC, NBC, and CBS simultaneously, I looked next to me and—wouldn't you know it—there stood Jamie.

Because she was between me and the doorway to the room, I knew that once the news was over, I would be presented with two options: introduce myself to her or awkwardly ignore her as I left the room. I chose the former.

> The last thing she wanted to do was to go to a party to meet "a bunch of dumb jocks."

"Hi, my name is Orel Hershiser," I said, using my very best cool-but-not-too-cool-to-appear-too-interested voice.

She looked at me quizzically and laughed. "That's not really your name. What's your real name?"

Now it was my turn to laugh. "That *is* my real name."

Frowning just a little to let me know she wasn't sure if I was still kidding, she changed the subject. "You're on the team?"

"Yes," I said. "I'm a pitcher."

"So, when are you going to turn professional?"

> She looked at me quizzically and laughed. "That's not really your name. What's your real name?"

I liked this question because it gave me a chance to look good. "I am a professional. Believe it or not, we get paid to play." Then, knowing what she was really asking, I added, "I'm hoping to make it to the big leagues in a couple of years."

Then it was my turn to change the subject. "Didn't you love that Shrimp Paesano?" (Having seen each other several times helping ourselves to the caterer's specialty, we already had something in common.)

Of course, she said that she did and our conversation was off and running. I could tell that Jamie was very bright. I liked that about her. She told me about her love for the arts and her interest in singing. I told her about my family and how much they meant to me. I found out later that she liked that about me.

I was having a great time. What had started out to be a nice but probably forgettable evening at the team owner's home was turning out to be filled with major potential.

As Jamie and I talked, I noticed that some of my teammates were noticing her, too. My guard went up immediately. Knowing this, I didn't dare leave Jamie's side. Not for anything. Not for a minute . . . not even to go to the bathroom.

In a little while, Jamie introduced me to her mom, Angie Byars. She was very personable. I think it was Angie who had noticed the team bus in front of the Turner's home because she offered to give me a ride home.

I said yes.

In about thirty minutes we left the party. As we were driving to my apartment, Angie offered to drop herself off first so Jamie could take me the rest of the way by herself. I liked this idea.

When we reached the apartment, I asked Jamie for her phone number. "I'd like to call you when we get back from the road trip," I said. She found a piece of paper and jotted her number on it.

When I leaned across the console and reached out my hand to take the number, Jamie wasn't sure if I was trying to shake her hand or give her a good-night kiss. She pulled back a bit while I fumbled to take the slip of paper.

It was the only awkward moment that night.

I thanked her for the ride, got out, and walked—almost jogged—into my apartment building without looking back.

Months later Jamie asked why I gave up so quickly on the idea of kissing her good night. I reminded her that from my introduction—"Hi, I'm Orel Hershiser"—until she had handed me her phone number, I had not let her out of my sight . . . not even to go to the rest room.

WE DO

To say that Jamie and I saw each other a lot over the next few weeks wouldn't begin to describe it. I was completely taken by her. Almost every waking minute we were together or talking on the phone. I loved how Jamie wasn't just a "yes person"—how she asked such good questions and challenged my thinking. She was so poised and I loved her sense of humor. I was especially excited because of our similar faith experiences. One night I told her that on June 2, just three days before the party at Tom Turner's, I had prayed and asked God to "lead me to a girl some day who loved Him and wanted to follow Him as much as I did."

Jamie Byars was the answer to my prayers. On July 31, six weeks after we began dating, I asked her to marry me. (I wish our sons didn't know that part of the story!) She said yes. And on February 7, 1981, six months later, Jamie and I were married.

Less than eight years later, in December of 1988, after both of our sons had been born and my career and family had exceeded my wildest expectations, my mom wrote me a letter. In addition to congratulating me on my performance in the play-offs, she wrote: "Thanks to Jamie for her kindness . . . you make a great team."

When your mom—especially a mom like mine who loved her kids and sacrificed everything for them—tells you that, you have done well!

There's no question that, without Jamie, I would not have had the career I had in baseball. And her support hasn't only been as my wife and the mother of our sons. She's even stood in as my battery mate.

Soon after we were married, I went through a phase where I struggled horribly with my control on the mound. It was my first major slump and I was despondent. Jamie kept after me and encouraged me.

One night she went to my dresser drawer and pulled out a pair of socks. She rolled them up and threw them to me across the room. "Come on, you can figure this out," she said, offering to catch me.

Can you imagine my wife pretending she's Johnny Bench? It was awesome. A *Sports Illustrated* writer who heard about this story called those pitches, "argyles, low and away."

When she agreed to marry me, just a minor-league baseball player, Jamie put her own life on hold. Given the plans and dreams she had for a career in music, this was no small sacrifice. But we made the decision that we'd work together to see if I could make it to the bigs. Jamie definitely kept up her end of the bargain.

She committed herself to providing everything I needed to

stay focused on the game. Even though I had excellent representatives, Jamie was the front line of defense, protecting my schedule from anything that could distract me. In private, we confided in each other as best friends. In public, she carried herself with kindness and grace. This was no small thing, especially as my career heightened and the demands of being married to a famous person brought significant challenges for her.

> Jamie Byars was the answer to my prayers. On July 31, six weeks after we began dating, I asked her to marry me.

A meticulous person, Jamie held the countless details of our family together. Even now, I can see her with calendars and baseball schedules spread out on the kitchen table, coordinating school activities and road trips so the family could be as much of a unit as possible during the season. For many years there were rental houses, moving boxes, and hundreds of other arrangements made to turn these places into "homes." And she did it without complaining. Jamie became a master at creating a loving and warm environment for us no matter what the circumstances.

After my retirement in June of 2000, Jamie's challenges changed. Someone has said that a retired husband is a wife's full-time job! I hope that's not true with us.

Instead, my promise is to find ways to turn the tables on Jamie—helping and supporting her after so many years of her sacrificing for the boys and me. Knowing how much she loves to sing and how gifted she is, I encouraged her to sing at our church's Christmas concert during our first post-retirement holiday season. It was wonderful to sit in the "stands" and be her fan—to support her where she is so gifted.

My mom was right. We do make a great team. Jamie was, and still is, the answer to my prayers.

THE BOYS

The changes Jamie and I made when we got married didn't compare to the massive adjustments that having children provided. Quinton and Jordan brought us tremendous happiness—and a complete reversal of our lifestyles. If you have kids, you know what I mean.

These babies slipped into our lives and demanded our time and our attention. They also took a toll on our sleeping habits. So we—especially Jamie—made the adjustment. Having children was important to us and we wanted to do our best at raising and nurturing them.

> Jamie became a master at creating a loving and warm environment for us no matter what the circumstances.

The day-to-day details of being a good father were—and continue to be—a tremendous challenge. For this, I've done what I've always done: sought out good coaches. I have looked for men who have older children who have turned out well. I have watched them. I have asked them questions about being a good father and I've done my best to follow their advice and examples.

As the boys have grown, I have tried to keep the communication channels open, asking them what I need to do to be a better dad. Learning to keep short accounts in baseball between my coaches and me has helped me to avoid letting too much time pass between conflicts and resolutions with my sons. This has been very helpful.

I know that I'm their coach. There are times when all they need is cheering from the dugout. At an early age, my coaches discovered that they could motivate me better with a pat on the back rather than a kick in the pants. I know this is true for our guys, too.

> These babies slipped into our lives and demanded our time and our attention.

At other times, my role gives me the responsibility of challenging them, instructing them, and disciplining them. If my coaches and trainers had not done this for me, I could have legitimately questioned their professional skills and their belief in me. Not ever wanting my sons to doubt my love or my resolve, this is also true as I face the challenge of being a good dad.

Finally, I am learning that my job as a dad is not to squeeze Quinton and Jordan into my personal agenda, but to encourage them as they pursue their own God-given talents and dreams.

One of the most important things I am learning is the priceless value of our family. Certainly, this includes my parents, my sister and two brothers and their families. But it is especially true of my own family.

An evening just hanging out together can be total pleasure. Enjoying each other's company is one of the greatest experiences in life.

MEMORABILIA VALUE

For the past twenty years, I have collected baseball memorabilia. For example, I have several cases of baseballs from the '88 World Series—autographed by the Series MVP! I have the hat and jersey I was wearing when I broke the late Don Drysdale's record with fifty-nine consecutive scoreless innings. I have an artist's illustration of four Dodger pitchers—Sandy Koufax, Don Drysdale, Fernando Valenzuela, and me—personally signed by each of us.

I have signed, game-worn jerseys from Wayne Gretzky and Mario Lemieux, a putter Arnold Palmer used, and football memorabilia signed by Walter Payton and Jerry Rice. I even have a piece of the hardwood floor from the old Forum where the Lakers used to play.

Why does this memorabilia have value?

These things represent never-to-be-repeated events, so they have historical value. Because they are rare they can bring a significant price—a price that someone is willing to pay.

Like the value I placed on making it to the big leagues when I was a kid, Jamie and I have set our own goal to have a great family. Like a collector who predetermines what he's going to accumulate—all Cy Young winners or Hall of Famers—we have made a conscious decision to do our best to "gather" those things that have high value for our family.

And doing this once isn't enough. Placing value on these things is something we have to do and redo, decide and redecide, day after day. This ongoing challenge is something we work on constantly. It shows up in our scheduling choices, the way we deal with crises, even the tone of voice we try to use. Faced with things that pull at us, we are trying to stay committed.

Sometimes this isn't easy. But the genuine love we have for each other and the great times we have together remind us that it's worth it.

"TO US, HE IS DAD"

On Christmas morning, just a few months after I had retired from baseball, our older son, Quinton, presented me with the finest gift I have ever received from him.

Being the son of a well-known person is challenge enough. But to be the offspring of a famous baseball player and be named Orel Leonard Hershiser V can be formidable. Quinton (Latin for "five") has handled this very well. From the time he was very small he has been his own man. And Jamie and I have encouraged him where he has personally excelled. He has successfully pursued areas where I hardly have a clue—computers, music, drama, and media production.

Because of his talent, expertise, and love for these things, Quinton used the editing equipment at school and produced a video for me. On Christmas morning 2000, I opened a small package marked "To Dad. Love Q."

> Like the value I placed on making it to the big leagues when I was a kid, Jamie and I have set our own goal to have a great family.

Our family took an immediate break from opening presents and gathered around the television to watch what Quinton had produced.

Set to a bed of classical music, the first few minutes of the video included some of the highlights from my career. This was familiar footage to all of us. The music and the visuals were skillfully woven together. I was amazed at how well Quinton had captured the emotion of these scenes.

Soon the screen went black and these words appeared in white:

To the world, he's Orel Hershiser, but to us, he is Dad.

The rest of the video showed highlights of the early years of our marriage. We saw clips of Quinton and Jordan as babies. We watched them running through the house with Batman capes and tumbling in the backyard. Under the video scenes was Mark Schultz singing "He's My Son." Once more, a song said it best.

I'm down on my knees again tonight
I'm hoping this prayer will turn out right
See, there is a boy that needs your help
I've done all that I can do myself

His mother is tired
I'm sure you can understand
Each night as he sleeps
She goes in to hold his hand
And she tries not to cry
As the tears fill her eyes

Can you hear me?
Am I getting through tonight?
Can you see him?
Can you make him feel all right?
If you can hear me
Let me take his place somehow
See, he's not just anyone
He's my son

Sometimes late at night I watch him sleep
I dream of the boy he'd like to be
I try to be strong and see him through
But God, who he needs right now is You
Let him grow old
Live life without fear
What would I be
Living without him here
He's so tired and he's scared
Let him know that You're there

Can you hear me?
Can you see him?
Please don't leave him
He's my son.

Now the boys had outgrown these backyard antics. Those days were long gone, but it was awesome to visit them again.

Not only was the video masterfully produced by the Q-Man,

but it reminded me of the career highlights I really care about. The career from which I will never retire.

The video ended with the screen reading "Merry Christmas, Dad." I walked over and hugged Quinton. Tears of joy and thanks rolled down my face. (When I do this, Quinton calls it "crying like a woman.") As Robert Fraley had challenged me, at the end of my career I loved my wife and my kids knew who I was.

This is better than any World Series trophy.

MY FAVORITE THING ABOUT DAD

On my forty-first birthday, September 16, 1999, I squeezed in a quick trip home for the celebration. The Mets had an off day and we were close enough to Orlando that I was able to jump on a plane and make it to central Florida for a few hours. It was my first birthday party at home in several years.

As we sat at the table enjoying a great home-cooked dinner (nothing on the road could ever compare to Jamie's kitchen) with my family and a few close friends, someone suggested that we "go around the table and tell Orel what we appreciate about him"—verbal birthday presents.

This took me by surprise and before I could object, everyone agreed to the idea. So they started. Ordinarily this would have been embarrassing, but these were people I loved so I sat quietly and took it all in.

When we got to our son Jordan, who had turned eleven the day before, he couldn't think of anything to say. Jamie encouraged him, "It's okay, Jordan. Just say something you love about Dad."

This is better than any World Series trophy.

After a few more moments of silence, Jordan spoke in a voice we had to strain to hear. Without looking up, he whispered,

"The thing I love about Dad is the way he gets over bad things."

No one around the table said anything. The impact of Jordan's words had struck a chord with everyone. Especially me. I knew that his words were about the importance of maintaining balance and integrity in spite of adverse circumstances. Even at age eleven, he had noticed my honest attempt to not bring my work home—especially my failures. And, unlike most sons, as a batboy Jordan often had the chance to see his dad make mistakes from the dugout or even in video replays on TV!

As a gifted athlete and student, I'm sure that Jordan will face plenty of failures and disappointments on the field, in school, and in life. I want him to continue to learn how to treat others with respect no matter how poorly his day has gone.

THE FAMILY

If you're a Pirates fan, you'll never forget the 1979 World Series. The Bucs took the Series by defeating the Baltimore Orioles in seven games. Willie Stargell, the Pirates' dominant first baseman, gave his team a nickname.

Stargell told the press that this team would always be known as "The Family."

However, within a few years, this family, like every other major-league baseball team, had been picked apart by retirements and trades. They may have called themselves family, but like every team I played for, they were eventually dismantled. That's the way it is in baseball.

BASEBALL'S TOUGH LESSON

There was something very special about the chemistry among the 1998 Giants. Although I only spent one year with the team, we became very close. During downtime on the road, we hung out together, going to movies or dinner. This was a special group of guys. The camaraderie was honest and fun.

Darryl Hamilton was one of the reasons we were so close. Not only did he have a great sense of humor, but Darryl was one of the team leaders, someone the guys really respected.

Midway through the season, we weren't quite living up to expectations on the field. We called a team meeting to talk it over. After the meeting, some upper-management people called a handful of us together. Darryl and I were in this meeting. The San Francisco brass wanted to tell us a couple of things: the Giants were counting on us to help them lead their team into the play-offs, and those of us in this meeting—unless something completely unforeseen happened—would not be traded.

> What is true in baseball, where players are traded and replaced at a moment's notice, does not have to be true in our homes.

We left the meeting with a renewed enthusiasm and resolve to make the play-offs.

A few days later, Darryl Hamilton was called into Dusty Baker's office. It's not that unusual for a player to be asked to meet with a skipper, one-on-one, but there was something about the tone of his voice and the look on Dusty's face that clued us in.

Darryl was in Dusty's office for only a few minutes in which Dusty explained to Darryl that something completely unforeseen had happened and that he had been traded to the Colorado Rockies. Darryl was to pack his bags and report to Denver immediately.

I remember the look on Darryl's face as he walked back into the clubhouse. He didn't say a word. He didn't need to.

Although we understood the way these things happen in

baseball and that there was no one to blame, the fact that our friend had just been sent packing tore us up. I can still see many of my teammates, especially the guys who had been part of that meeting, hugging Darryl and shedding some tears.

Making the play-offs or not, we were really going to miss Darryl.

But this is *not* the way it has to be in *real* families. What is true in baseball, where players are traded and replaced at a moment's notice, does not have to be true in our homes.

I know this may sound old-fashioned and outdated, but there's nothing on earth that's more valuable to me than my family. They'll never be traded. That's a promise.

I love my family and I challenge you to do the same.

"THAT'S OKAY, HONEY; WE'LL SURVIVE"

Throughout my whole career, there were lots of weighty negotiations and important meetings that forced me to examine my priorities and motives. Life was serious business. But right in the middle of it, something happened that still makes me laugh. Quinton dropped a doozy on us.

Kids have always looked to their dads to provide them safe harbor. When they're threatened, you hear them calling to their friends, "Oh yeah . . . but my dad can beat up your dad." Their dad's strength bolsters their own confidence.

Quinton was only four years old when the Dodgers made me the highest-paid player in the history of the game. Q should have had the safest harbor, but for some reason he wasn't taking it that way.

Three years later I was no longer the highest-paid in baseball, but was still the highest-paid player with the Dodgers. One afternoon, Jamie was picking Quinton up from school. She knew something terrible had happened because of the look on his face as he walked to the car. Tears were streaming down his cheeks. Once safely inside the car, Quinton let it all out.

"What's the matter, Q?" Jamie asked. "Why are you crying?"

Between sobs, Quinton told his mom how the kids at school had teased him and how they had said "a bunch of mean stuff."

"What were they saying?" Jamie responded, expecting the usual first-grade fare.

"They said that my daddy is the highest-paid player on the Dodgers," Quinton wailed. "That's what they said." He took a deep breath. "It's not true, is it, Mom?"

Jamie couldn't believe it. Our son was actually upset with my new contract. But Jamie treated the situation with tenderness.

"Yes, Honey, it's true. But don't worry. Next year it'll be Darryl Strawberry, not Dad."

"Really?" Quinton said between sighs.

"Yes, really," Jamie smiled.

PRINCIPLE #8

Live with Gratitude

How does a man adequately say thank you? This is something I want to keep trying to do. I have a deep sense of gratitude because I have been on the receiving end of so many good things.

I've already mentioned a lot of reasons I'm thankful. But one of my favorites was reaching an important milestone in 1999.

"SHOOT ME UP LIKE A HORSE"

I signed with the Mets in '99 for several reasons. First, they had a solid bullpen. I knew there weren't too many complete games left in my forty-one-year-old arm and I was going to need some help finishing games. Plus, they had a great offense, with guys like Edgardo Alfonzo, Robin Ventura, John Olerud, and Mike Piazza.

Playing in New York where the fans and media would demand a lot from me was something I was also looking forward to. Pressure like this was always a great motivator.

I started the season with 190 career wins and, with all these things going for me, I also thought I'd have a good shot at reaching two hundred.

On July 22 in Montreal, I finally reached that goal. This put me in an elite group of major-league pitchers (I became the ninety-ninth) to reach two hundred victories and I was very thankful. But, believe it or not, getting to 199 wins was even better!

Nine years before, on a cold spring night in Dodger Stadium, when I had walked off the mound after getting bombed by the Cardinals, I had logged exactly ninety-nine career wins. I had done everything I could to get to one hundred, but the terrible pain in my shoulder wouldn't let me continue. As it turned out, surgery and rehab prevented me from throwing another pitch for over a year. Making it to one hundred victories would now be an even bigger goal to reach.

The next spring, as my rehab progressed, I remember joking with Dr. Jobe. I said, "I don't care if you have to shoot me up like a horse . . . I've got to get that hundredth before I'm done."

Dr. Jobe smiled and shook his head. He knew that I was kidding, but he also knew how serious I was about getting to this milestone.

Now, nine years later with the Mets and 198 career wins under my belt, I started at Shea against the Expos. This was not a normal outing. I had pitched two days before—July 4—against Atlanta and had gotten killed. The Braves had brought plenty of their own fireworks to New York. My short outing had put a lot of pressure on the pitching staff so the next day in the clubhouse I volunteered to start against Montreal with only one day's rest. Bobby Valentine agreed.

> Believe it or not, getting to 199 wins was even better!

New York City was in the middle of one of those East Coast heat waves, with the temperature at game time still in triple digits; it didn't take very long to get loose in the bullpen. Although the stifling heat actually helped with the aches and pains, conserving my energy would definitely be a priority.

Having 198 career wins meant that I had won ninety-nine more games since 1991 when I had teased Dr. Jobe with "shoot me up like a horse." On this suffocating night, I had a chance to win more games after shoulder reconstruction than I had won before—something no one would have ever predicted.

Three hours later I sat in the clubhouse doing post-game interviews. Most of the reporters wanted to talk about the victory—I had pitched five scoreless innings and gotten the win. Some of their questions included how, at almost forty-one, I had been able to hold up in the sweltering heat with only one day's rest. Most of the questions had to do with reaching two hundred on my next outing.

But one well-prepared reporter asked me about the significance of 199 wins. To me the real story was winning one hundred games since the spring in 1991 when I would have been happy to have just nailed one more post-op victory. With this victory, I had won more games since the surgery than I had won before. Talk about being thankful.

CELEBRATION AND GRATITUDE

When I watch sports, I enjoy seeing how athletes celebrate. Everyone has his own style. They show their exuberance in different ways.

Kirk Gibson's double-pumping fist as he ran between first and second after his clutch home run to win the first game of the '88 Series will always be etched in my mind. I was part of the mob of Dodgers standing at home plate to welcome Gibby home as he rounded third. As Vin Scully said, "In a year that has been so improbable, the impossible has happened."

But when I look at the videotape of my own celebrations

during the '88 post-season, I see a reserve in my initial reaction to the victories. Over the years, people have asked about those first few minutes at the close of the NLCS and the World Series. Was I surprised or in shock . . . or what?

> With this victory, I had won more games since the surgery than I had won before. Talk about being thankful.

By now you know I have always seen myself as fairly normal. All along, I knew I'd have to work hard to succeed in baseball. It wouldn't be handed to me.

Throughout my career, one of the things I tried to do was to treat every game—even the most critical ones in the post-season—as "just another game." *I'm not going to change anything,* I'd repeat to myself as I prepared for a start. The challenge wasn't to rise to an occasion. The goal was to stay the same. Even in play-off situations, I wasn't going to change my approach to the game.

But in 1988, when everything came together in a way I couldn't have imagined, I was pretty overwhelmed. With the thrill of having been on the mound for the last outs in both the NLCS and World Series, instead of instantly celebrating like a boy opening that Christmas present he really wanted, I was filled with the deepest sense of gratitude you can imagine.

I'm not criticizing other forms of celebration, especially when they come naturally and are not meant to taunt the opposition. But, for me, it was as though I couldn't believe what had just happened . . . and that it had happened to me.

When I struck out Howard Johnson to finish off the Mets in the seventh game of the NLCS, I dropped to one knee. It was an instant of unplanned expression of thanks, genuine humility before God. (Although it was good that I didn't stay down very long or I would have been crushed by my teammates!)

Just over a week later, the fifth game of the World Series ended when I struck out Oakland's Tony Phillips. We won the World Championship and, for me, every boy's dream had come true. There was a delayed reaction . . . from concentration to celebration. My hands dropped to my sides and I looked up. Although I had hoped and dreamed of this moment, I was in shock and completely exhausted.

> Instead of instantly celebrating like a boy opening that Christmas present he really wanted, I was filled with the deepest sense of gratitude you can imagine.

But as I look back, I know that this was another moment of gratitude. I was saying thank you again.

Between that moment and boarding the plane in Oakland several hours later, everything was a blur. I hardly had a moment to think. The frenzy was unbelievable. On the plane ride back to LA, as Jamie and I had time to gather our thoughts, we kept saying to each other over and over again, "Can you believe it? Can you believe it?" What we were feeling is impossible to describe. We were amazed with what the team had accomplished. The experience of reaching this ultimate goal was mind-boggling.

Since that night, I have been asked by hundreds of people—reporters, men, women, and children—"What's it really like to win the World Series?"

In answering their question, I have thought about that plane ride from Oakland to Los Angeles and how Jamie and I felt. Of course, we were thrilled beyond words. Completely in awe. But this feeling is no different than when you make the honor role or watch your bride walk down the aisle or hold your own child for the first time or close a big business deal. You know that feeling.

Winning the World Championship was exactly the same . . . except that my experience was on television in front of a bunch of people. That is the only difference.

A TEAM EFFORT

I have talked about balance. So much of what I was feeling at these pinnacle moments was the tension between enthusiasm and humility—dedication to the process and gratitude for the results.

I have talked about focus and excellence: working hard to please my dad and my early coaches, living with self-discipline, trusting Dr. Jobe and Pat Screnar with my rehab, and being committed to Jamie and my family.

But this didn't happen in a vacuum. This was a team effort. There were others who made all of this possible and without them, it would not have happened. My success was not a solo performance and I was thankful for everyone involved.

During my years in the majors, I continued to ask for help. This was something I didn't outgrow. For example, there were times when I was tired and didn't feel like working out. I knew that I could have faked a workout and fooled my coach or therapist. I often talked to them when I arrived at the ballpark. I'd tell them that I wasn't "into it" and wanted them to follow me around in my workout to be sure I was doing it right.

They could have shamed me into thinking that, as a veteran, I shouldn't need this kind of supervision. But they didn't. It was their job to help me and there were days when I needed it.

I'm gonna bag it. I'm gonna fake it, I'd think to myself. *I'm gonna listen to music and pretend like I'm doing reps when I'm not.*

> This feeling is no different than when you make the honor role or watch your bride walk down the aisle or hold your own child for the first time or close a big business deal. You know that feeling.

"You've gotta walk me through this and motivate me today," I'd admit to one of the therapists. "I need your help."

Even as a professional, success wasn't only about my hard work or ability. Far from it. It was the collective outcome of lots of people's skill and effort. How could I take all the credit?

BASEBALL'S GREAT FRATERNITY

Every active major-league baseball player worked hard to earn his way to the big leagues, but until I got there, the legacy of the game was being held up by someone else.

Now it would be my turn. This was a sobering thought.

One of the Dodgers' strategies was to make sure young players got a chance to meet as many legends as possible. Just being in their presence filled me with a great sense of the past and the responsibility we now carried. Johnny Podres, Sandy Koufax, Larry Sherry, Carl Erskine, Roy Campanella, and Don Drysdale weren't only great players, they also personified the great tradition of the game.

As I traveled, I met other veterans: Lou Brock, Bob Gibson, Johnny Bench, Mike Schmidt, Pete Rose, Hank Aaron, Willie Mays, Bob Feller, and Tom Seaver. These were Hall of Famers, baseball's elder statesmen, and they deserved my respect. They had built the reputation of the game. They were the foundation of our national pastime and the game I was now benefiting from. These men were members of baseball's great fraternity.

And it wasn't only the stars that I held in high regard. Some would say that a certain player wasn't part of the tradition if he never made an All-Star team or because he only hit .180 or never won twenty games. But I felt differently. Just because autograph seekers didn't mob these guys, they still deserved my respect.

Every man on the field is charged with preserving and furthering the integrity of the game. As a player, I was responsible for holding up my end of protecting this national treasure.

The rules of baseball saw it this way, too. Our salaries in the regular season were different, but in the play-offs, all twenty-five men on the active roster got paid the same. Every single player wearing a uniform had earned it. In the same way, every man who played the game made a contribution, regardless of his stats. As major-league baseball players—win or lose, visible or invisible, hero or goat—we all contribute to the great heritage of the game. And I'm part of that.

Success . . . was the collective outcome of lots of people's skill and effort. How could I take all the credit?

This amazing fact still astonishes me.

PERSPECTIVE

But there were more reasons for my gratitude than what I experienced performing between the lines.

Every major-league team has an annual Family Day. All the players' kids get to come on the field for a "game." I loved bringing my boys to the ballpark when they were young for these special outings. Seeing children in official baseball attire swinging bats and running around the bases is always a lot of fun. Jamie and I have some wonderful scrapbook pictures of Quinton and Jordan as little boys in Dodger uniforms. (Imagine trying to fit "Hershiser" across a two-year-old's jersey!)

One of the benefits of staying in the game longer than most players was that our sons grew into young men while I was still active.

Can you imagine my gratitude at having Q and J share my days at the ballpark with me? During the month of August in 1998, Quinton—at thirteen—took every road trip with me . . . just the two of us. The Giants "employed" the boys as clubhouse kids. They also spent some time that year—and the next with the Mets—as batboys.

In fact, Jordan was in the dugout during the entire fifteen-inning marathon play-off game against the Braves in 1999. This was a game I'll never forget. We were battling for our lives, having already lost three games to Atlanta. Bobby brought me in from the bullpen with two men on and one out in the fourth inning.

After getting the Mets out of the jam and pitching two more scoreless innings in relief, I spent the rest of the game in the dugout. I was able to be Jordan's assistant batboy for eight innings—until Robin Ventura ended the game with a line drive over the right center field fence to keep our play-off hopes alive. I remember that a heavy mist fell off and on all night, creating a surreal glow to the stadium and adding to the drama. And my son was right there with me for the whole unforgettable experience. This was Jordan's favorite day in the bigs . . . and one of mine, too.

Very few men my age get to share their careers with their kids. It just isn't practical to take them along to the office or to the shop every day. But because I was in baseball, I got to do exactly this—including the drives to and from the park.

Spending this kind of time with my sons was a rarity in baseball life. Having them be a part of my professional life reminded me of my role with them. Including them in my work made me even more thankful to be their dad—something from which I'll never retire.

THE OVERFLOW

One of the responsibilities and benefits of being a professional athlete was being given the chance to give back. Over the years I was grateful for the opportunity to bring happiness to those in need and, of course, it was wonderful to be able to share this with my family.

I'm sure you've seen ads for the United Way during NFL games. You might see a great big linebacker sitting on a tiny chair at a low table with little kids or a famous quarterback holding a youngster. Over the years, I have also gotten involved in charity work. This has been very fulfilling.

Just before the 2001 Super Bowl, Jim Nantz did a short interview with George W. Bush. His closing question seemed to catch the new president off guard. "Do you have a message for the almost one billion people watching you right now?"

President Bush paused for a moment, then smiled. "Yes, Jimmy," he said. "Love your neighbor." I love the simplicity of this powerful truth.

Although Jamie and I supported many national charities, my favorites were those efforts that helped people who were close by. I loved the personal contact.

When we were in San Francisco, I regularly met with inner-city kids—honored guests of the Giants—before games. The Giants had special baseball caps made with my name and number on the side and each of the kids received one of the caps. These times were great. And over the years, I have visited many kids in hospitals or corresponded with young people who had been struck by a disaster.

> I was able to be Jordan's assistant batboy for eight innings.

Why did I, along with many other professional athletes, take part in these activities? The answer is pretty simple: I had the ability to help, I believed that it was my duty, and my conscience didn't give me a choice.

Helping out also filled me with thankfulness. It is better to give than receive.

LOOKING UP

And like so many other good things I get credit for, this attitude was a gift from my parents and grandparents. Their unselfishness toward me and my siblings and their loving spirit toward everyone—neighbors, mechanics, plumbers, and ministers—was respectful and kind. I just followed their example.

Because I had seen my Grandpa Gillman leaning over the car fender and listened to his thoughtful remarks—"Wow, I would never have seen that"—I learned the joy and power I had to brighten someone's day.

As a professional athlete, my world was filled with many wonderful people. Although there were times when I was tempted to drive past them without speaking or walk past them without looking up, the example of my mentors wouldn't let me do it.

"Hey, Joe," I'd say when I'd pull my car into the players' parking lot. "How ya doin'?"

He'd smile and wish me luck, "Get a win for us today, Bulldog."

I'd park my car and walk past Joe Schwartz on the way to the stadium door. "Hey, if you ever need anything," I'd say, "just let me know. I know the rules about you asking for autographs, but you're not asking. I'm offering."

Joe would thank me. I appreciated what he was doing for me and my teammates and I knew he could tell.

Walking through the bowels of the stadium on my way to the clubhouse, I'd often pass vendors who were hard at work, carrying stock to their stations to get ready for the game. "Hi," I'd say as we passed each other. I didn't make a big deal of this, I just wanted them to know that I knew they worked hard to get the stadium ready and they deserved my respect. They always seemed to appreciate it.

As a professional athlete, my world was filled with many wonderful people.

My world was filled with people who were there to make my life easier. With every encounter, I had a chance to make a contribution to their day. This was a privilege and I didn't want to waste it.

I HADN'T FORGOTTEN

I remember how it was to be a teenager, pumping gas at the Exxon station in Cherry Hill. Once in a while, someone would pull into the station, driving a collector 'Vette or a classic T-bird. Sometimes guys from out of town would whip into the station, driving a Lamborghini or a Maserati. I remember how I felt as the drivers stepped out of their cars. At that moment, these men had a chance to make my day.

"Can I help you?" I'd say to them, looking eager and very helpful.

"Sure, fill it up with high test," some would say, smiling and looking me in the eye.

"Can I do the windshield?" I'd offer, hoping I'd have a chance to actually touch this car.

"That would be great. Thanks."

And I'd clean the windshield enthusiastically.

"Can I check the oil?" I'd ask. A yes was a huge thrill.

After checking, I'd be sure to wipe my fingerprint smudges off his hood.

Without knowing it, that man had made my day.

But if the guy got out of the car, kept his head down, answered me with a grunt, didn't speak to me while I pumped his gas, then ripped the receipt off the plastic holder without even looking at me, he had missed the chance.

Amazingly, just a few years later, although I didn't feel that much different than when I was pumping gas at the Exxon, I was a "star." I could be like the guy driving the Lamborghini. And I had the power to make someone's day. People may not have expected it from me, but in my opinion, they deserved it.

The Bible calls this being "salt and light." Just a pinch of salt can change a bland food. Just a little light can brighten a dark room.

In being kind, I was giving these special people the power to make a contribution to my day, too. People like DiMag.

As an ex-military man and a former railroad worker, no doubt Carl DePhillipo had once been a tough guy. Now, close to the age of my dad, he loved to serve. He got his nickname from hanging around Joe DiMaggio. For years he'd offer rides to ball players, often taking guys who hated to fly from city to city. Guys like Mickey Mantle, believe it or not.

> I could be like the guy driving the Lamborghini. And I had the power to make someone's day.

DiMag lived in Cleveland and frequently offered to give me rides to and from the airport or the Jake (Jacob's Field). He wasn't a manager. He wasn't a coach. He wasn't a player. DiMag wasn't even an Indians' employee. But he was like a permanent fixture at the Jake—a guy who loved being with the players and loved doing things for them.

In watching DiMag work around the clubhouse, run errands for people, and hang out just in case someone needed something, I wanted to thank this guy. I wanted him to know that I noticed his kindness and was grateful.

"Hey, DiMag," I'd say. "What can I do for you? How 'bout lunch tomorrow?"

And in wanting to do something for DiMag, I found a lot of happiness. His genuine caring for Jamie and me, his enthusiasm, and his genuine love for baseball were infectious. I was thankful for DiMag. His example of selflessness and humility motivated me. We became good friends.

A GRATEFUL HEART

Outside of baseball there are lots of people in your life and mine who serve us: the receptionist at the office, the clerk at the grocery store, the mailman . . . The list is almost endless.

And, like I had in baseball, we have a choice. We can look at the floor—refusing to make eye contact and risk getting involved—or we can get involved. We can live in isolation or we can make room for these people in our hearts.

There's an ancient Asian custom that when you give a gift to a person you truly love, you present the gift with both hands. This is a symbol of not holding anything back. When I heard of this tradition from Dr. Craig Barnes just a few months after I retired from baseball, I remember thinking, *I want to be a two-handed gift giver . . . and a two-handed gift receiver.*

The secret to happiness is to give and receive with a grateful heart, holding nothing back. In good times when the world was thrown at my feet, and in difficult times when getting through the day didn't seem possible, I tried to set my mind on this.

> We can live in isolation or we can make room for these people in our hearts.

With all that I have said about my drive to perfect the process that prepared me for baseball, some might think that I didn't take the time to reflect on the gifts I'd received. This is not true. Actually, I did my best to be grateful while I was in the game. Some old-timers told me that they only realized what they had in baseball after they retired. I did my best not to wait. I wanted to appreciate the experience while I was still in the midst of my career.

TRUE BLUE

I'll always be thankful to the Dodgers. Yes, I spent three excellent years with the Indians and had a great year with both the Giants and the Mets. But it was the Dodgers who made the call in June of 1979 and gave me a chance in the big leagues. And it was a Dodger uniform I was wearing as the World Champions in 1988. I will always be grateful to the organization no matter what.

In November of 1994, on the threshold of being a free agent, I received a call from Fred Claire, the general manager of the Dodgers. He wanted me to meet with Peter O'Malley, the owner of the Dodgers, and himself the next day. We agreed on a time. That night Jamie and I discussed all the options we could think of. A long-term deal? A short-term deal? No deal? We prayed that God would give us wisdom.

The next morning, I walked into the meeting room. Fred and Mr. O'Malley were already there. They stood and greeted me warmly.

Fred began to ask questions about what I wanted to do for the 1995 season. I told him that I felt strong and wanted to continue to pitch. Without being rude at all, Fred let me know that he didn't think that there would be an opportunity for me to pitch with the Dodgers for the 1995 season. As a thirty-six-year-old, the Dodgers weren't sure that I'd have much more to contribute.

I told Fred and Mr. O'Malley that because of the lock-out situation they had not been able to see me practice. But I said that I was throwing as well as ever and knew that I could still get big-league hitters out. I wasn't ready to quit. They understood and wished me well.

As I left the meeting, I remember how I felt. I was disappointed, for sure. But I was not angry. I was sincerely grateful to the organization, and nothing was going to change that. Baseball was filled with uncertainties. Peter and Fred were businessmen and had to make the call as they saw it. I understood.

> Peter and Fred were businessmen and had to make the call as they saw it. I understood.

Over the next few days, the sports pages were filled with stories of my departure. Reporters called and asked if I was retiring. Others asked why I was leaving Los Angeles. I jokingly told them that I didn't usually hang around places where I wasn't welcome. But because I was—and would always be—thankful to the Dodgers, there was no criticism in my voice.

And regardless of the fact that many big-league pitchers retire by age thirty-six, my dream was big enough to include several more years of effectiveness. What had happened so far was more than I could have ever imagined and I wasn't ready to walk away. I knew that I could still pitch and that I just needed to find a team who needed me. I didn't panic. Yes, I was a Dodger born and bred and I knew that playing for someone else was going to be a huge change, but deep down I believed it would work out.

From the day of the meeting with Fred Claire and Peter O'Malley until I retired in 2000, I won seventy more games. I went to the play-offs four times, won the MVP of the American League Championship Series, and played in the World Series two more times.

Am I boasting? Absolutely not. The years with the Dodgers were just as wonderful as the final years of my career. And I took each year . . . one at a time . . . as a gift. And since these were gifts, my job was to receive them gratefully—with both hands.

THE DOXOLOGY—A REPRISE

Six years after the meeting with Fred and Mr. O'Malley, I was sitting back in the dugout at Dodger Stadium. But the situation was completely different than when I was there in 1988.

I had spent the last seventeen years living a dream.

Instead of being on the threshold of doing something no major-league pitcher had ever done—become the MVP of both the NLCS and the World Series—I had just walked off the field for the last time. I had given up eight earned runs in less than two innings. I had lost the ability to do my job effectively. Davey had come to the mound to take me out.

Now, sitting in the dugout, I could see Davey Johnson standing on the mound where I had just been, talking strategy with Carlos Perez, who had come in from the bullpen to try to salvage the game I had started.

Even though well-wishing teammates and coaches surrounded me, I felt completely alone. Well, actually, not completely alone. The words from my presurgery press conference came flashing back, "The God who was with me in 1988 is the same God who is with me right now." I knew this was still true. And I had spent the last seventeen years living a dream.

Scanning Dodger Stadium, I carefully soaked in what could be my last view from the dugout as a big leaguer. I closed my eyes and quietly sang to myself.

Praise God from whom all blessings flow.
Praise Him all creatures here below.
Praise Him above ye heavenly hosts.
Praise Father, Son, and Holy Ghost.

Leaning my head back on the familiar cement wall behind the bench, my heart was once again filled with gratitude.

PRINCIPLE #9

See the Signs

On most of my days in the big leagues, I watched the game just like you. When I didn't start, my time was spent in the dugout. I enjoyed the camaraderie of my teammates. And I especially loved the strategy of the game.

> *With no outs in the bottom of the eighth, we're down by a run. Our lead-off man drills a first-pitch line drive into right center for a single. The crowd gets going. They want a rally. Knowing that the guy on first isn't a base stealer, the manager nods to the rookie sitting at the end of the bench—not a lot of major-league experience, but lots of big-league speed.*
>
> *The manager signals to the home-plate umpire, who calls time-out. The rookie sprints across the infield to first base and the veteran trots back to the dugout to the appreciative cheers of the hometown crowd.*
>
> *Our teammate in the on-deck circle slowly walks toward the batter's box. In that moment, the third-base coach glances toward the manager in the dugout. Making no eye contact with his coach at third, the manager looks at his lineup card, then scopes the flag*

in center field. He adjusts the bill of his hat with his thumb and forefinger. Putting one foot on the first step of the dugout, he touches the end of his nose with his index finger. He claps his hands and shouts some encouragement to the hitter walking toward home plate. Then the manager folds his arms across his chest.

Just before getting to the batter's box, the hitter stops and looks down at the third-base coach, who slides his right hand down his left forearm, tugs at his right earlobe then touches the end of his nose. He repeats these motions adding one final touch to the bill of his hat, then claps his hands together.

With one foot on the bag, the rookie at first is doing some stretches and deep-knee bends. But, like the hitter getting ready to step into the batter's box, his eyes are glued to the third-base coach. The first-base coach stands next to the rookie, resting a hand on his shoulder.

The pitcher circles around behind the mound, rubbing up a new ball. He glances at the shortstop, who moves a few feet toward second. The batter steps in, the rookie takes his lead, and the pitcher steps onto the rubber. He looks down to his catcher, now crouched behind home. The catcher makes a quick glance to his dugout, drops his right hand in front of his upper thigh, sticking his pinkie to the right. He wiggles all four of his fingers, taps his thigh, and puts his little finger out again.

The pitcher nods and goes into the stretch.

For most of the forty thousand people in the stands, this is just an exciting moment in the game. They've looked up from their nachos long enough to cheer the base hit and see the pinch runner move to first. More savvy fans understand that the manager is making some moves to give his team a good chance to score. But the few baseball fanatics watching from their seats know that the last minute has been jammed with some intense strategic communication.

For the players on the field and for those of us in the dugout, we saw the signs and we knew what they meant. Like two chess masters, the managers had assessed the situation, considered the skills of their players, and set a specific play in motion. Now it was time to execute.

SIT NEXT TO ME IN THE DUGOUT

Not only do I love the strategic part of baseball, I also enjoy revealing it to my friends. If you were able to sit next to me in the dugout, I'd love to show you the things that most fans completely miss—the game inside the game . . . the strategy and the signs.

I'd explain that our manager knows that the reliever on the mound has just about reached his maximum pitch count. But he's guessing that the manager in the other dugout is going to try to squeeze one more hitter out of him. We've got a left-handed hitter on deck and he's on a hot streak, especially with men on base. The opposing manager wants to save his left-handed reliever for our lefty.

Between innings, the manager gave our lead-off hitter a heads up. "Keep an eye on the first pitch. I know this guy. He's tired. I'd say he's going to try to sneak a first-pitch fastball past you for a strike. Be ready to jump on it."

As the hitter steps out of the dugout, the manager gives him a shout of encouragement. Then he walks over to the bench coach. "Get the rook ready. If we get on base here, I want him to run."

The bench coach walks to the far end of the dugout and has a talk with the speedy rookie. "Loosen up," he says. "If we get a hit, Skipper wants you to run."

Sure enough, we get a fastball on the first pitch and a solid line-drive base hit.

When the manager looks down the bench and nods to the rookie, it's not a surprise. He's ready to go.

Before the next hitter steps into the batter's box, he stops and looks down to the third-base coach. Knowing our hottest hitter, who's been deadly with men in scoring position, will be up next, everyone's expecting a bunt. Our manager knows what everyone's thinking, especially the opposing manager.

> If you were able to sit next to me in the dugout, I'd love to show you the things that most fans completely miss—the game inside the game.

But if we bunt, the manager thinks to himself, *then they'll walk our best bat with first base open. I've got to see how this develops.*

He adjusts the bill of his cap. The first-base coach and the third-base coach know what this means with no outs and a man on first: "Pay no attention to the bunt sign I'm about to flash. Fake the bunt."

The third-base coach slides his right hand down his left forearm. "Fake a bunt." The hitter knows that the rest of the signals are a decoy. Tugging on his earlobe means "Bunt." The manager is hoping that the other skipper picks this one up. He's been using it all night.

Sure enough, the first and third basemen draw in.

Hoping the pitcher tries to get cute and keep the batter from having a good pitch to bunt, our manager is hoping for a ball.

The first-base coach rests his hand on the rookie's shoulder. "Take your lead but do not steal."

He squeezes three times. *"Do not steal."*

The opposing catcher looks into his own dugout. His manager folds his arms across his chest. "Low and away."

The pitcher walks around behind the mound, rubbing up a new ball. He's going low and outside on a right-handed hitter. He figures that the bunt is going down the first-base line. If not, the ball will probably be hit to that side, behind the runner. An almost undetectable nod moves his shortstop a few steps toward second.

The pitcher walks up the mound, steps on the rubber, looks in to get his sign, and goes into the stretch. He checks the rookie taking a generous lead off first . . . and delivers.

Our hitter squares around as if to bunt, then pulls the bat back. Ball one.

One pitch can be pretty complicated, just like life.

MISSING THE SIGNS

Whole chapters—even whole books—have been written on the signs and strategies for a single baseball game. Whether we're on offense or defense, there's almost always something going on. Managers are signaling to coaches. Coaches are relaying those signs to hitters and base runners. Catchers are flashing signs to their pitchers. Pitchers are moving their infielders around with a glance and a nod. This is a game filled with a lot of important communication.

But what happens when a player misses a sign? Or worse, what happens when he ignores one? Because missing signs can completely throw off the morale of the team and the rhythm of the game, most clubs have fines as reminders. Some managers will bench a player or air him out after the game, especially if the missed sign was critical to the outcome of the game. The price for ignoring a sign can even be more severe.

> Whole chapters—even whole books—have been written on the signs and strategies for a single baseball game.

Even though many players make more money than their manager does, every one of them is under his authority. This doesn't mean that to be effective he must be overpowering or rude. Good managers maintain their leadership with confidence and skill.

We may disagree with the manager's decision. We may even lose a game because he makes the wrong call. But it's our job to pay close attention, follow his direction, and learn.

BEING INTENTIONAL

The first—and most important—principle in this book reminds us that our coaches (parents, managers, teachers, bosses) are the most important people in our early lives when it comes to the development of our skills and character.

When we're young, most of these coaches are given to us. We don't have a chance to choose them. But in every case, there is something to be learned. Their signs and signals are not subtle. They tell us what to do or what to avoid—what works and what doesn't work. Their good judgment shows us the way. And as long as we're listening carefully, their mistakes can be just as instructive.

As we grow, we get to choose some of our coaches—friends, mentors, and even authors of our favorite books. Some of these people are our equals, but because we know that we have something to learn from them, we listen and learn.

Baseball is a team sport. Disregarding our teammates' signals can be just as dangerous as ignoring the ones from our manager or coaches. In life, paying attention and learning from our peers is a mark of real maturity.

Tommy Lasorda used to tell us that there are three kinds of people in the world: those who make things happen; those who watch things happen; and those who stand around and say, "What happened?"

The secret to making things happen is to live intentionally and on purpose. Between the team meetings—where we learned the signs—and the game, the challenge was to memorize the signs, anticipate the signs, then be ready to pick up the signs. At work, your boss, your coworkers, and your subordinates are constantly communicating with you. The words they speak and the things they don't speak are worth paying close attention to. Learn, anticipate, and pick up the signs.

> In life, paying attention and learning from our peers is a mark of real maturity.

If you're married, you know about the nonverbal signals you receive from your spouse. The look on their faces and the subtle tone of their voices usually mean something. If we're not paying attention, we could miss the sign—the nuance of the moment—and waste a great opportunity.

If you have kids, you know about signs. A shrug or a grunt or a slammed bedroom door means something. If we're too busy with our own schedules or zoned out because we're tired, we could miss the signals. And these can be the most opportune times to parent. Learn, anticipate, and pick up the signs.

I'll admit that doing this well is a lot of work for me, too.

SEE THE PROBLEM

A professional athlete's life is filled with full-service help and lots of creature comforts. The league made the playing schedules so we don't have to be concerned with where we're supposed to be going. Our day-to-day itineraries were handled by the team's traveling secretary and our accommodations were first class. My workouts were directed by the trainers and therapists. Clean uniforms were always hanging in my locker. Even my towels got picked up by clubhouse kids.

It was possible to drop into a zone and not even think about any of these things. These conveniences gave me energy to concentrate even harder without distraction. But it was not an opportunity to go on autopilot.

I didn't want to let these comforts dull my attitude, my focus, or my preparation. The principles in this book came from a determined effort to be intentional about my career—to avoid laziness at all costs. I also tried to pay close attention to my body. Eventual retirement was not optional; it was a certainty. I was doing my best to stretch out my productive years, so I listened to a tender elbow or a sore hip or late-inning fatigue. Dozing off and missing these signs would have shortened my career and lowered my effectiveness. And I knew it.

> If we're too busy with our own schedules or zoned out because we're tired, we could miss the signals.

But outside of baseball, reading the signs is a more difficult challenge. You know that from the time they were available on cars, I have had a GPS as standard equipment. Missing road signs and getting lost is one of my strong suits. I need to hear that friendly electronic voice: "Straight on." "Turn left in three hundred yards." And the very familiar, "When possible, make a U-turn."

I know that unless I work at it, I'll get caught going in circles rather than moving toward my destination. In my car, I have to trust that voice because if I don't, I'll probably get lost. In life, I want to see the signs and stay on target.

EXECUTE THE MESSAGE

In baseball, you pay attention to the signs and you carry out the instructions. My goal was to execute the message. In other words, get the job done!

When I was in the batter's box and the third-base coach signaled for a hit and run, I was not a hitter up there to check out the velocity and location of the next pitch. I was a hitter whose only job was to put the ball in play, no matter where it was thrown.

When I was a runner at first base and I got the steal sign (this didn't happen very often), I'm not a base runner that's taking his normal lead. I'm a base runner that's stealing. My only thought is, *What do I need to do now to get a good jump?*

When I was on the mound and the manager wanted a pitchout, that was the sign. I may have disagreed with the call. I might not have thought the runner on first was going to steal. But my manager had made the decision so I made the adjustment. I didn't continue to execute or do what I thought. The sign changed everything.

A sign had been sent and my job was to do my best. I needed to follow the instructions and make the play. Not paying attention or ignoring a signal would have created a serious problem.

In the same way, most people pay attention at work or at school. The goal of getting good grades or a promotion on the job motivates us and keeps us on our toes. But the greatest challenge is seeing the signs and doing something about them in the other areas of our lives.

> Outside of baseball, reading the signs is a more difficult challenge.

Unlike baseball, a lot of the day-to-day signals are unplanned, unfamiliar, and new. When they come from someone I respect or someone I love or a source I trust, I'd better pay attention. I need to make the necessary adjustments. If I disregard the signal, I may miss out on a valuable opportunity.

Through my years of growing up and then playing baseball, this was one of the ways that I learned to compete and win. It

> But my manager had made the decision so I made the adjustment. . . . The sign changed everything.

was a constant challenge. What I lacked in overpowering strength and dominance could be overcome by paying attention to the signs and submitting to the wisdom of others.

My baseball experience has helped me to develop a relationship GPS. My natural tendency may be to not pay attention, but the subtleties of baseball have made me more aware of what's going on around me. I may notice a person's facial expression or try to find out what's behind what they've just said.

My GPS may say, "Person is fearful; say something encouraging."

Are they anxious and uncomfortable? "Person is stressed; make him laugh."

Do they want me to back off? "Person is preoccupied; don't take it personally."

Or are they ready to go deeper? "Person needs a listening ear; stop what you're doing and focus."

In baseball, some of the signs were unintentionally sent. An anxious hitter in a pressure situation often sent a message that gave me a chance to benefit from his nervousness.

In life, many of the signs are also unconscious. Capitalizing on them gives me a chance to get to the truth, solve a problem, or reassure someone. When Jamie asks me if I like her outfit, she may really want to know if I'm looking forward to going out with her. When one of the boys is critical of himself, he may be challenging me to reassure him and defend his self-respect. In business, when a colleague seems overly sensitive about his project, he may be looking for constructive input without a personal attack.

I'm thankful for what I learned in baseball about recognizing signals and making the appropriate adjustments. And I know that recognizing problems, seeing the signs, and daring to adjust are going to be lifelong tasks—no less challenging than playing in the big leagues.

THE TABLE BACK IN THE CORNER

I began this book by suggesting that this would be a conversation between you and me. As we've gone along, I've pictured us eating lunch together, sitting on those vinyl benches in that booth back in the corner of our favorite diner.

I have let you in on some of the principles that are very important to me. It's also been a lot of fun to review my past and be reminded of these things.

If you and I had met at our diner when I was still a major leaguer, you may have wondered how we could relate. But even though I was a professional athlete, you now know that I have always thought of myself as very normal. We've actually had a lot in common.

Or course, you may look at me and say, "You've had a great career. And you've got the trophies and plaques to prove it. Not only do I not have any trophies, I don't even have a trophy case!" What I would say to you is pretty simple. Yes, I have been very fortunate. I have lots of awards and personal memorabilia. But the trophies I care about are the principles I've talked about here. They are the ideas, the lessons, the examples, and people who have been a part of my life. We can have these things in common, even if no one has ever asked you for an autograph or your name has never appeared in the newspaper.

You know that honesty—brutal honesty—has surrounded me and you know that I've picked up the habit. There has been honest evaluation and self-evaluation. I have forced myself to learn from the past and apply it to the present. Although some accuse professional athletes of acting childish, this is an adult process.

I want to avoid the extremes of preachiness or of beating

around the bush, but my challenge to you is to learn what I learned in baseball. Recognize the situation, see the signs, and risk doing something about it.

If my weight was out of whack, it affected everything in my performance. If I faked my workouts and my strength wasn't up to par, it affected everything about my performance. If I allowed bad habits to control me, it affected everything about my performance.

> The trophies I care about are the principles I've talked about here.

Baseball was great Spring Training for the rest of my life.

So, if I live like the Lone Ranger and refuse to seek the advice of people I respect, it will affect everything. If my relational skills are calculated and self-centered, it will affect everything. If my priorities are out of balance, it will affect everything. If I take myself too seriously, it will affect everything. If I neglect my family and forget to be grateful, it will affect everything.

And if I stop paying attention to the signs that will let me know that these things are in need of repair, I'm going to be in serious trouble.

Since we do have a lot in common, I want you to join me in the adventure of living a full life. That means that when we're faced with a challenge we'll have the guts to do something about it, even if we've been locked into it for years. We'll ask for help, we'll listen, we'll weigh the cost, we'll execute, and we'll refuse to give up.

I know we can do these things.

Thanks for your time. And thanks for lunch. It's been great.

> Baseball was great Spring Training for the rest of my life.

Orel Hershiser: Baseball Statistics

CAREER PITCHING STATISTICS

Year	Age	Team	AL/NL	Wins	Losses	Appear	Starts	Completed	Shtouts	Saves	Innings	Hits	Runs	HR	Walks	Strkouts	ERA
1983	24	Dodgers	NL	0	0	8	0	0	0	1	8.0	7	3	1	6	5	3.38
1984	25	Dodgers	NL	11	8	45	20	8	4	2	189.7	160	56	9	50	150	2.66
1985	26	Dodgers	NL	19	3	36	34	9	5	0	239.7	179	54	8	68	157	2.03
1986	27	Dodgers	NL	14	14	35	35	8	1	0	231.3	213	99	13	86	153	3.85
1987	28	Dodgers	NL	16	16	37	35	10	1	1	264.7	247	90	17	74	190	3.06
1988	29	Dodgers	NL	23	8	35	34	15	8	1	267.0	208	67	18	73	178	2.26
1989	30	Dodgers	NL	15	15	35	33	8	4	0	256.7	226	66	9	77	178	2.31
1990	31	Dodgers	NL	1	1	4	4	0	0	0	25.3	26	12	1	4	16	4.26
1991	32	Dodgers	NL	7	2	21	21	0	0	0	112.0	112	43	3	32	73	3.46
1992	33	Dodgers	NL	10	15	33	33	1	0	0	210.7	209	86	15	69	130	3.67
1993	34	Dodgers	NL	12	14	33	33	5	1	0	215.7	201	86	17	72	141	3.59
1994	35	Dodgers	NL	6	6	21	21	1	0	0	135.3	146	57	15	42	72	3.79
1995	36	Indians	AL	16	6	26	26	1	1	0	167.3	151	72	21	51	111	3.87
1996	37	Indians	AL	15	9	33	33	1	0	0	206.0	238	97	21	58	125	4.24
1997	38	Indians	AL	14	6	32	32	1	0	0	195.3	199	97	26	69	107	4.47
1998	39	Giants	NL	11	10	34	34	0	0	0	202.0	200	99	22	85	126	4.41
1999	40	Mets	NL	13	12	32	32	0	0	0	179.0	175	91	14	77	89	4.58
2000	41	Dodgers	NL	1	5	10	6	0	0	0	24.7	42	36	5	14	13	13.14
Career Totals				204	150	510	466	68	25	5	3130.4	2939	1211	235	1007	2014	3.48

POST-SEASON PITCHING STATS

Year	Round	Team	Opponent	Games	ERA	Win-Loss	Saves	Complete Games	Innings	Hits	Runs	Walks	SO
1985	NLCS	Dodgers	St. Louis	2	3.53	1-0	0	1	15.3	17	6	6	5
1988	NLCS	Dodgers	Mets	4	1.09	1-0	1	1	24.7	18	3	7	15
1988	WS	Dodgers	Oakland	2	1.00	2-0	0	2	18	7	2	6	17
1995	ALDS	Indians	Boston	1	0	1-0	0	0	7.3	3	0	2	7
1995	ALCS	Indians	Seattle	2	1.29	2-0	0	0	14	9	2	3	15
1995	WS	Indians	Atlanta	2	2.57	1-1	0	0	14	8	4	4	13
1996	ALDS	Indians	Baltimore	1	5.40	0-0	0	0	5	7	3	3	3
1997	ALDS	Indians	Yankees	2	3.98	0-0	0	0	11.3	14	5	2	4
1997	ALCS	Indians	Baltimore	1	1.29	0-0	0	0	7	4	1	0	7
1997	WS	Indians	Marlins	2	11.70	0-2	0	0	10	15	13	6	5
1999	NLDS	Mets	Arizona	1	0	0-0	0	0	1	0	0	0	1
1999	NLCS	Mets	Atlanta	2	0	0-0	0	0	4.3	1	0	3	5
12 Post-Season series totals and averages:				22	2.65	6-3	1	4	131.9	103	39	42	97
3 World Series totals and averages:				6	4.07	3-3	0	2	42	30	19	16	35